John
Author of God H

SILENT HOPE
LIVING WITH THE MYSTERY OF GOD

SORIN BOOKS   Notre Dame, IN

John Kirvan is the author of *God Hunger* and *Raw Faith*, both companion volumes to this work, and of the highly successful *Thirty Days With a Great Spiritual Teacher* series, a library of fourteen books which offer the wisdom of the mystics for daily meditation. He currently lives in southern California where he writes primarily about classical spirituality.

© 2001 by Quest Associates

www.sorinbooks.com

International Standard Book Number: 1-893732-41-X

Cover design by Angela Moody

Cover photo www.photodisc.com

Text design by Katherine Robinson Coleman

Interior photos: www.comstock.com 41, 57, 73, 89 ,105, 121, 137, 153, 169, 185; www.corbisimages.com 25; www.photodisc.com 9, 7, repeated boxed tree images.

Printed and bound in the United States of America.

Library of Congress Cataloging-in-Publication Data

Cataloging in Publication Division
101 Independence Ave., S.E.
Washington, D.C. 20540-4320
Library of Congress Cataloging-in-Publication Data
Kirvan, John J.
Silent hope : living with the mystery of God / John Kirvan.
        p. cm.
        ISBN 1-893732-41-X (pbk.)
1. Mysticism. 2. Hidden God--Meditations. I. Title.
BL625 .K575 2001
291.4'22--dc21

                                                    2001002439
                                                    CIP

SILENT HOPE

In memory of my father and mother.

As always for F. B.

In a special way for
Paul, Ronald, and Norma,
my brothers and sister.

With thanks to Robert Hamma
for once again
calling these pages to order.

CONTENTS

PART ONE

A Journey Into God's Silence

To be religious
is to believe that it is meaningful
to speak into the endless desert
of God's silence.

—KARL RAHNER

In the beginning there is a hunger for God.

Then in time there comes a realization that the God for whom we hunger is unknowable, that this God escapes our every attempt to confine him to the limits of our mind and soul. This God is accessible only to raw faith.

But there is still another discovery to come. The God for whom we hunger, the God in whom we believe is a silent God and there is no escape from her silence.

There is only hope.

**

I was very young when I set out on a journey to meet God. Some said they had seen the God I was seeking. But I had not. I never have. Some said they had heard that God speak. I had not. I never have. But in the beginning, and ever since, God has been a hunger that won't go away.

Not then. Not now.

I think often of Kiriloff in The Possessed. *"All my life I have been haunted by God," he said.*

I have come to accept that this haunting, haunted journey would never be, can never be, a path of easy certitude and satisfaction. It will always be a way of unfathomable mystery and contradictions. I have come to know that this is a journey that demands raw faith in what is uncapturable and unknowable, an embrace of mystery that cannot be approached in any other way than by surrender, by letting go of security and certitude.

But above all else I have come to understand that I would have to live with the silence of God. There have been sightings, glimpses, whispers. But after all these years he remains unseen, her silence goes unbroken. There are hints, hauntings. A moment of presence. A moment of absence. Someone here, someone there, no one here, no one there. Presence, absence. Something. Nothing.

Everywhere, in everything, in everyone, there is only God's silent, mysterious presence. The journey that begins in hunger, that is sustained by raw faith, is lived out in hope.

We cannot make God speak. We cannot break her silence. We can only hope that in the silence of our journey we will find the God for whom we search, who beckons us on, who permits us to hope.

***

The critical moment of our spiritual journey comes with an act of hope, when however afraid of the dark we may be we choose life beyond what we know, can ever know.

It is a moment of dissatisfaction when we choose not security but risk, not the familiar but the unknown, when we surrender to a hunger beyond curiosity for whatever lies beyond the doors of our lives. We choose whatever awaits us in the next room, realizing that as long as we sit warming our souls by the fire we are only half-alive.

It is not an easy choice, for however dissatisfied we might on occasion be, however imprisoned our soul, however God hungry, we are more likely to choose comfort than courage. The mustiest old room is still home. We can find our way around it without bumping into the furniture. Its comfort and predictability enclose us. And on the other side of the door, in the world "outside," who knows what?

But at some point we must cross its threshold, no longer content with half-a-life. Chances are that we will do so "hoping" that God will speak to us out of the darkness and make it all clear, that he will embrace us and make it all "better."

But the hope on which we will build, through which we will grow will not be a blind optimism. Rather it will be an act of courage to go on journeying in the face of God's silence.

Our spiritual journey will not be a return to Eden, but a passage into mystery.

We need to know and accept, however reluctantly, that the God for whom we hunger, who exerts his attraction from the other side of the door is a silent God who pursues us silently in a noisy world. She will forever remain beyond our understanding. We need to know and accept that the mother tongue of this mystery is silence.

His silence will not end. Her mystery will not dissolve. Taking our first steps into this silence and mystery is never easy. For one thing we carry the baggage of "gods" accumulated and treasured along the way.

An avuncular God whom we are sure we discarded with our childhood turns out to be still tucked away in our hope chest. A white-bearded good-guy-God on whom we have counted to "throw" a ball game or an election is still around.

And when we are hurting unbearably we still go looking for a "fixer" God: someone to cure a wounded marriage or snatch from death someone we cannot live without. In our most bloody, barbarous moments we turn on a God who has failed to cure cancer or disarm a holocaust of Jews, gays, and gypsies.

Our silent God, it turns out, is not an interventionist. Or a magician. Or an infinitely powerful social worker. She is a God who is most conspicuously silent when we most desperately want to hear her voice, to see and feel her presence, to experience her influence.

Loaded down with inherited expectations we may find this divine "absence"—this silence—incomprehensible to the point of cruelty. It can frighten, discourage, and even embitter us. We have a right, we feel, to a God who is more understanding, more human, someone who acts more in the image of our own best instincts. We may want to deny it intellectually, but we go on finding it hard, if not impossible, to accept and trust a God who does not do for us what we would do for ourselves if we could. We want a God who we can understand, who understands us. Who responds to our pain with cures we prescribe. Who speaks when spoken to, if it is only in language of our contrivance.

Instead we get a God who turns our disappointments upside down, who plunges us into the very silence that we have sought to break through—who makes his silence the point of our disappointment. Who expects us to hope.

"We expected to understand you. Instead you insist that we embrace your mystery."

"We expected to hear your voice. Instead you have responded with silence."

For many this is intolerable. Some of us respond by taking God off our screen. We retreat back into the musty spaces where we were comfortable. Or we jury-rig a God with whom we can live comfortably, who delivers what we need at any given moment. But these are not options if you believe that spirituality is not about remaking God but about transforming ourselves, by living beyond what we can comprehend, by living in hope.

We have to build a transformed life around mysteries wrapped in silence.

We have to let God lead us into that world of what cannot be understood, defined, or captured in words, where the only possible language is silence, where our only hope is hope itself. To trust any other language would lead us back to that musty old room, to that half-world where we are doomed to place our hopes in an understandable God who is no God at all. Such a God is but an idol fashioned by our imagination to provide an explanation for what cannot be explained.

"God is never an explanation," said Rabbi Abraham Joshua Heschel, and is "always a challenge."

We are in the short and long run disappointed, not because our expectations are too great, but rather because they are too small.

God insists on being God, and insists too that our God hunger not be reduced to worshiping an idol made in our own image and likeness. We don't have to settle for an idol. A burning bush awaits us in the darkness. But how do we live with the darkness, with the silence?

We live in hope.

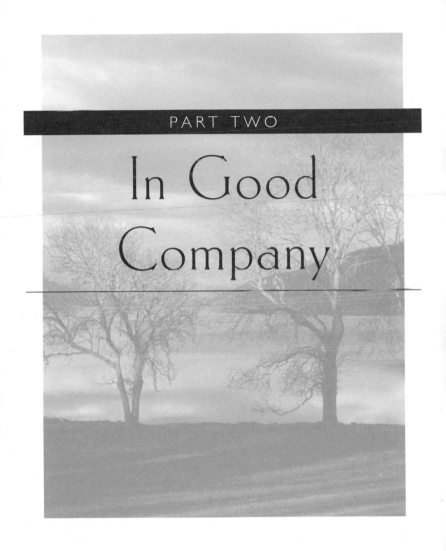

PART TWO

In Good Company

When we take pride in our wisdom
we become, as St. Paul warns, "fools."
For all of the world's wisdom
and all of our skills
contrasted with the wisdom of God
is utter ignorance.

So if we count on our own wisdom
to bring about union with God
we are truly ignorant
and we will never reach our goal.

If we are to enter into God's wisdom,
we will do it by unknowing
rather than by knowing.

What we consider light
must become darkness.

—JOHN OF THE CROSS

I listened one afternoon to Isaac Stern talking about his hero, Pablo Casals. The genius of the great cellist, he said, was his ability to open wide a door into gardens of extraordinary beauty, of unimaginable color, of scents beyond comparison. Casals, he said, was generous with his invitations. But it was always up to his guests to accept his invitation and to decide how far into the garden they would go.

That's what the great mystics do.

They describe spiritual beauty and spiritual pain they have known and paths they have followed into worlds of extraordinary beauty—and of equally threatening darkness. They open doors. They offer their hand. They offer to come with us.

But each of us still has to choose how far into the garden, how deep into the mystery we will go, how far our hope will carry us. For the garden that is opened to us is planted in silence and nourished in solitude.

It is a demanding journey, not of the mind but of the soul. Our ideas will have to surrender to wonder. Our words will have to become a pathway into silence. What little light we have will end in the darkness and silence of a God who escapes our every effort at definition.

But with the great mystics as our companions it need not be a lonely journey. With them we are invited in the pages that follow to explore ten basic elements of classical western spirituality—what it is like to enter the garden, what it is like to live in hope with a silent God.

It is not, however, an intellectual exploration but a spiritual one. These meditations are meant for praying, for unwrapping the mystery, for pulling back one veil at a time, knowing with each hope-filled, tentative gesture that the veils are without number, the mystery beyond plumbing.

There is no special order to the themes that are reflected upon. You can approach them as you choose. They are so many arrows pointing at an indefinable center of mystery.

This exploration, however, if it is to lead anywhere, must be conducted with our hearts open, from that place within all of us that Dag Hammarskjöld calls "a center of stillness surrounded by silence." What we seek on our journey is not a solution to a problem, not the answer to a question, but an encounter with the mystery of hope that will by very definition far exceed the best efforts of our mind, the utmost limits of our imagination.

We are not asked to abandon our intelligence or surrender our sanity, but to rely on the tools of the spirit, several of which are employed in the exploration of each theme.

Each section is introduced with an "epigram," a meditation-provoking passage taken from the writings of a great spiritual teacher. You might do what I did. As I read the works of the great mystics, a passage would leap out at me. There was and is no way of predicting which passage, or why this passage and not another. On another day, perhaps it might have been another passage. No matter. I would stop and pray it through. In this book I invite you to do the same. Be aware that in prayer you never need be alone. You bring someone with you—one of the great mystics whose words and life have inspired the words you have just read. I have added a short reading that develops the epigram and introduces the life and times of the teacher, the world in which they experienced God, and the unique characteristics of their experience. What is important to understand is that these short passages are not meant to tell the whole story of their lives and sanctity, but just to create a doorway large enough to let us into their lives.

Then come five exercises for the soul, each designed to involve us in the three great classic prayer forms of western spirituality.

There are "mantras," short, pithy, often epigrammatic sentences, that by way of paradox and irony catch the essence of a great spiritual truth. They are easily committed to memory and often make their impact by constant repetition.

There are short spiritual readings—meditations. It is a form of prayer that best allows us to summon up silence, to focus our wildly work-family-news-distracted souls. These meditations, although prompted by the words of a mystic, are my own. They are not meant to summarize the insights of a great teacher. They are not a substitute for reading their words, for directly contemplating their experience of God. They are merely a record of how one person responded to something they said. You will have your own response. Trust it.

And finally there are short intercessionary prayers in which we speak directly to the God whose presence we celebrate. Some would say that this is the most revealing of all our prayers, for in this moment we speak to the God in whom we truly believe. The one we address, as someone has said, when nobody else is listening. You may use the words provided but your own, by definition, will be more revealing, more searching. Note too that even though these prayers are cast as night prayers, you can pray them whenever you are looking for words to center your day.

How should you use these exercises? Any way you want. On any schedule, at any interval that is convenient, comfortable, and/or rewarding. Do the meditation in the morning, if you prefer, and the prayer at night. Or the whole thing in one snatched period of quiet. Do what you want. But do exercise an element of regularity. Without it you could miss out because of mere forgetfulness or laziness. Or because you just don't feel like praying today.

But we must not forget as we explore the experience of those who have gone before, as we exercise our own souls in this pursuit of mystery, that our personal quest for a living hope is at its depth a unique moment in history. Millions have preceded us. But this is the first time God and we have met. There has never been anyone quite like us. There has never been a spiritual moment quite like this. One of the great theologians of this century, Karl Rahner, puts it this way: "Each individual man or woman is a unique and unrepeatable term of God's creative love. Each must find their path to God in a way that is proper to themselves."

Be prepared, in any case, to be surprised, because no one is more surprising than God. We may in the end, as the Kabbalah says, despite our most careful planning and the most demanding discipline, "stumble" onto God. "Whoever delves into mysticism cannot help but stumble, as it is written: 'This stumbling block is our hand. We cannot grasp these things unless we stumble over them.'"

One other thing: do not look here for a map with a clear beginning, middle, and end. There are no straight lines from here to where your soul leads you, only a series of arrows pointing to a center that is mysterious, that is in the end as it is in the beginning, as it is at every step along the way—incomprehensible.

But always there is hope.

A Cloud of Unknowing

ANONYMOUS,
FOURTFENTH CENTURY

Our intense need to understand
will always be a powerful stumbling block
to our attempts to reach God in simple love,
and must always be overcome.
For if you do not overcome
this need to understand
it will undermine your quest.
It will replace the darkness
which you have pierced to reach God
with clear images of something
which however good,
however beautiful,
however Godlike,
is not God.

—*THE CLOUD OF UNKNOWING*,
FOURTEENTH CENTURY

The Unknowing

Over six centuries ago a nameless young seeker setting out on the next stage of his spiritual journey sought advice from a nameless older monk. The young man could no longer live at a distance from God.

It was a fortuitous moment for us all. For his request gave birth to *The Cloud of Unknowing*, an extraordinary introduction to the highest reaches of spirituality that remains to this day accessible and helpful to the God-hungry seeker at every step along the way.

For one thing this unknown fourteenth-century teacher makes clear that those "highest reaches" are not restricted to the spiritual elite. God doesn't have an "A" list. Her invitation to a spiritual life is universal, an idea not as widely accepted as we might have presumed or hoped. For many spiritual teachers over the centuries sanctity has been exclusively for the few and the chosen. The rest of us would just have to rein in our hopes.

The Cloud of Unknowing tells us to go for it. Nowhere does the old monk say: "This is not for you . . . only the spiritual elite need apply." The highest reaches not only call to us, but are open to all of us.

The old monk also tells us that it is God all the way to God. God doesn't stand waiting for us till we reach the heights. God is no less present to us beginners on the first day of our journey than he is to those whose journey has brought them to the soul's highest possibilities.

We experience God from the very beginning of our journey. But as we penetrate more deeply into *The Cloud of Unknowing* the experience gets deeper, more mysterious, more enveloping of our heart and our imagination.

At every stage of our journey we come to realize ever more deeply that even the best efforts of our intellect cannot take us where our heart wants to go, because only hope goes there. Our spiritual journey is in the beginning as it is in the end a journey of the heart.

The Unknowable

This journey of the heart is above all else a story of what we leave behind, a story of security lost and hope embraced. There comes a time, the old monk tells us, "to look ahead and forget what is behind you, time to pay attention to what you still need and not what you already have."

What we already have is what we know. What we look forward to in hope is the unknowable, to a God who is an ever-deepening silence, an ever-expanding mystery.

Every step into *The Cloud of Unknowing*, therefore, is matched by a step into a cloud of forgetting, a step away from all we have come to depend on, away from everything we thought we could know about the God for whom we hunger, a hopeful step deeper into silence, into mystery.

We have to accept that we cannot comprehend, cannot grasp the God for whom we hunger in silence and mystery. We have to accept that this is a journey that only hope can make.

Recognizing and accepting that our intellect cannot take us where we wish to go, we have to make, as a friend has written, "an intellectual decision not to use the intellect but to be present solely in the will, in the longing, in the thirsting, in the loving of the mystery of God."

This reversal of expectations, this surrendering of what we have come to trust will not, cannot, happen overnight. It requires not only our determination but our hope.

But as the older monk assures us, our hope is justified: "God who is our maker forever escapes our power to know. But he is forever accessible to our power to love. The power of love in each of us individually is great enough to reach him who is without limits, who forever escapes the power of our mind."

We cannot grasp God, but if we exercise our "power to love him, we will discover a love so powerful that it will bring with it all that God is." This does not mean that God will come into our life with blazing clarity and palpable warmth.

"Be warned that when you reach out to God in this simplicity you will find only darkness, the cloud of unknowing." No matter what we do this cloud of unknowing, of darkness and silence, of mystery accessible only to faith will always be with us.

But this "exercise of simple reaching out is the exercise that most pleases God."

I

God is calling you to something more.

—THE CLOUD OF UNKNOWING

There is no doubt about the spiritual goal that the old monk proposes to the young man—and to us. Simply said: it is an unbroken union with God, a union that puts aside, that forgets anyone and anything that comes between us.

The obvious danger is that in establishing this level of perfection as our goal—however much we may want to grow spiritually—we can be easily discouraged; not just in the beginning of our spiritual journey but even after we have made a few stumbling steps without managing to forget very much. Just about everything still seems every bit as important as it did before we started out, and God is still far from flooding our life and memory.

What we need to get straight from the start is that building a "cloud of forgetting" is not an overnight project. We are not going to go to bed some night loaded down with the world and good intentions and wake up the following morning having forgotten overnight everything but God.

Our culture is very big on overnight success. God isn't.

God remembers, even when we forget, that we succeed—and fail—one small step at a time. The perfect can be the enemy of the good . . . and too often is.

LET US PRAY

Let me fall asleep as who I am,

and awake

one small, uncluttered step

closer to you,

one small step closer to

the person I want to be.

It will be enough.

2

What matters is that you do not squander
your moments of silence and solitude.

—THE CLOUD OF UNKNOWING

One thing is certain about the spiritual path: it leads us, if
not directly, certainly inevitably, into silence and solitude.
And because very few of us are at ease with silence and
solitude, our first reaction may well be: "this isn't what I
had in mind."

We will then, if we are not careful—and for all the right
reasons—go about squandering the precious gifts that
have been given us. We will go about filling up the silence
and breaking through the solitude until they seem acceptable and fulfilling on our terms.

The "squandering" can be very subtle. It needn't be a
matter of recovering the noise of our work-a-day world.
It may be as simple as surrendering to a need to understand the experience, to find the right words for it, to cut
away at the mystery until we can grasp it. And we will
lose the silence in our effort to make sense of it.

Treasuring silence and solitude for their own sake is
never easy. Ask anyone who has attempted eastern meditation, or just a simple breathing exercise. The world
rushes in. Our brain and our heart are loathe to treasure
silence as silence, solitude as solitude. Loathe to let them
"just be." Loathe to abandon our need to understand.

LET US PRAY

Here in this night
let me know what it is
to be silent,
what it is
to embrace solitude,
what it is
to be present to you
without distraction,
without any need to understand.

Be still my soul.
Let me not squander
the gift of God.

3

God is waiting for you to do your part.

—THE CLOUD OF UNKNOWING

In trying to understand the spiritual journey there is always a tension between what we can do for ourselves and what we must leave up to God. *The Cloud's* author is very clear on the distinction: "Our task is the hard and unending one of putting behind us, of consigning to a cloud of forgetting all that must be put aside if we are to approach the cloud of unknowing, if we are to love God and God alone."

That's it. That's all. Getting out of God's way—clearing the ground is what we can do.

At the very minimum this involves ridding our lives of spiritually destructive behavior. But the hardest task is leaving behind the notion that there is something beyond this that we can do. There isn't.

"There are things that God and only God can do." And we have to let go and let God do them. "But if we work hard, if we press on in the task of leaving behind all that stands between us and God, then God, I promise you, will not fail you."

"But he is waiting for us to do our part."

LET US PRAY

Here in this night
let me be content
to do what I can do.
Let me get out of your way.

It will not be easy, I know.
I have spent a lifetime
getting in the way of
what is best for me.

Now you wait for me
to do my part
so that you can do yours.
But I will need your strength
to do even this.

4

Don't confuse spiritual desire with physical effort.

—THE CLOUD OF UNKNOWING

"It is easy," The Cloud's author reminds us, "for beginners to think of their spiritual journey in physical terms, believing that it is with brute physical strength and obsessive willpower that they will capture the ear and heart of God."

It is also easy—especially for beginners—to think that intense emotions are an important and inevitable companion on the spiritual journey, that there is a necessary connection between the intensity of our feelings and our closeness to God, that overwrought emotions are a sign of approval from a pleased God.

Both are just other versions of our common human conviction that union with God is a reward for our efforts, that spirituality is a triumph of willpower, that in the end it's all up to us, that spirituality's reward is "warm feelings."

Both are cases of "Hey, God, look at me." But we can't force God's hand. We can't change the fundamental truth that all is up to God. Muscularity and sentimentality don't cut it.

"Wait patiently on the will of the Lord with courtesy and humility, and do not snatch at it hurriedly like a greedy animal, no matter how hungry you are."

LET US PRAY

Here in this night

let me not mistake

what I want you to be

for who you are.

But rather

with patience

and humility,

seek out your will for me.

5

It is he that is at work.

—*THE CLOUD OF UNKNOWING*

The young monk for whom he was writing lived in a world that set great store by penitential practices that made room for God by getting the body out of his way. But to the young monk he said: "It does not matter how much you fast, what vigils you keep, how hard your bed, or rough your hair shirt."

We don't live in the young monk's world but one where bestsellers promise God and eternal peace in ten easy steps. To us he might say: "It doesn't matter what techniques you use, what schedule you follow, what program you rely on." It's all about love, about going where only love can take us.

It is surrendering to the God who is at work within us. Get out of his way. "Do not try to help him along, lest you spoil what he is attempting to do in and for you. You be the wood, he the carpenter; you the house, he its master."

All that is necessary is our consent.

LET US PRAY

Here in this night,

remind me again

of what doesn't matter.

It's not what I do.

It's you at work within me,

doing what only you can do,

doing all that can be done.

I give you my consent.

Amazement

ABRAHAM JOSHUA HESCHEL

The way to prayer
leads through acts of wonder
and radical amazement.
The illusion of total intelligibility,
the indifference to
total mystery that is everywhere,
the foolishness of ultimate self-reliance
are serious obstacles along the way.
It is in moments of our being faced with
the mystery of knowing and not knowing,
of love and the inability of love,
that we pray,
that we address ourselves to him
who is beyond the mystery.

—ABRAHAM JOSHUA HESCHEL

Amazement

Like everything else in our spiritual journey, living in hope is at the same time a life lived in the here and now and a life lived beyond mystery, a life lived with the silence of God.

For the post-Holocaust Jew, for the post-Holocaust gay and gypsy, for the whole post-Holocaust world, living in the here and now means living in the shadow of one of history's most terrible horrors. We live with the fear that it could happen again because we can't ever again deceive ourselves about human nature. If ever there was spiritual innocence it was lost in the ovens of Europe and the indifference of the race. "At no time," Heschel has written, "has the earth been so soaked with blood. Our fellow men have turned out to be evil spirits, monstrous and weird." Never was God more silent.

But if innocence was lost, there was something in the soul of Abraham Heschel that was not lost, that no one of us dare lose, if ever we hope to be whole again.

It is the phoenix-power of "wonder and radical amazement." You'll search in vain to find these virtues listed alongside the established canon of virtues . . . but they are the lifeblood of faith, of hope, and of charity. But especially of hope.

It is wonder and radical amazement that allow God to rise from the ashes, and our soul from half-life. Wonder sees what might be, what could be, despite what has been, what apparently is. Amazement is our willingness, our capacity to be surprised, to be caught off guard by the commonplace circumstances and events of our lives.

Together they testify that the horrors we have known, the evil that we are capable of cannot—must not—in the long run deaden our souls.

What is most amazing is that the case for wonder should be made by someone so close to the horrors of the Holocaust.

Abraham Joshua Heschel
(1907-1972)

When he was still a small child in Warsaw, Abraham Heschel would stand on a table surrounded by scholars and answer their questions with childish joy and unaccountable insight.

Decades later, on another continent and in a different language, he would become in the words of his daughter "a rabbi whose books were praised by Paul VI as helping to sustain the piety of Catholics; an Orthodox Jew with a white beard and yarmulke marching for civil rights and demonstrating against the war in Vietnam; an immigrant from Poland whose work is included in anthologies of exceptional English prose." He would come to number among his friends and co-workers Thomas Merton, Corita Kent, Theodore Hesburgh, Dan and Philip Berrigan, William Sloan Coffin and Martin Luther King, Jr. During the Second Vatican Council he would meet with Paul VI and with the Cardinals Bea and Willebrands who were shaping and shepherding the Council's document on relations with non-Catholic religions.

But between those moments in Warsaw and his teaching and activist years as professor of ethics and mysticism at the Jewish Theological Seminary in New York, the Jewish civilization into which he was born was all but eradicated, his mother, sisters, friends, and relatives murdered.

He would survive to live and grow and teach and write and inspire "in defiance of despair." There would remain with him "a feeling for the mystery of living . . . a sense of awe, wonder, and amazement" even in the wake of horror. But a feeling for mystery is not enough. "The root of religion," he would write, is "what to do with awe, wonder, and amazement."

He would translate his wonder into political activism and contemplative prayer. He would with unrelenting fidelity live out his Jewish heritage even as he insisted that "no religion is an island."

In a world of scholarship he would insist that "God is not a concept produced by deliberation . . . but an outcry from the heart and mind. God is never an explanation . . . always a challenge. It can be uttered only in astonishment."

In a world where God is too often sought as consolation and escape, he would insist that "God is an assault . . . a thunder in the soul."

In a world where we are tempted to find God guilty of our sins, he insists on wonder and amazement. When we are tempted to embrace religion for our sake, he reminds us that religion is for God's sake.

He would live to tell young people to "remember that there is meaning beyond absurdity."

I

The way to prayer
leads through acts of wonder
and radical amazement.

—ABRAHAM JOSHUA HESCHEL

At a time when we have become accustomed to having technological miracles served up with our morning coffee, it is hard to be amazed by anything. Which is to say, it is hard to pray.

The incredible speed and flexibility of our home computer and its move from our desk to our pocket is yesterday's miracle. "What have you done for me today?"

So except for triggering a plaintive plea for the world to slow down, amazement is not the stimulus to prayer that we have come to think of as essential. But it's the only one we have.

What it means is that—and this is a marvelous aid to prayer—we are going to have to look beyond Silicon Valley for our miracles, for the wonderful, amazing things that are just beneath the surface of our hour by hour world. We are going to have to look beyond and beneath the sign that says "genius at work" for the one that reads "mystery at work."

In the process we are going to discover that "acts of wonder and radical amazement" lead to prayer along a path shaped by hope.

LET US PRAY

You who are beyond mystery,
hear my prayer
as I walk as best I can
through the field of miracles,
that has been this day,
that will be, I pray,
this night,
and all the days to come.
Let me walk this path
shaped by hope,
colored by wonder,
and illumined by amazement.

2

Reverence is one of man's answers
in the presence of mystery.

—ABRAHAM JOSHUA HESCHEL

Reverence is the silence with which we greet the silent mystery of God's presence wherever we look. It is sensing a mystery at the heart of the world we live in. It is an acknowledgment that even the most commonplace can and should leave us speechless.

It is not, as we too often presume, an occasional ceremonial bow in the direction of the unusual, the exalted, or the merely proper, but rather a way of approaching the commonplace. It's an attitude that sees the hand of God wherever we look.

It is to walk in miracles. It is to stop and look. It is to be silent when words rush forward.

It is mystery consciousness that overcomes self-consciousness. It is the silence that is essential to God consciousness. It is paying quiet attention to what is there. "I was blind. Now I see." It is knowing that what we see is never all we get.

It is knowing that the surface of life is not all that there is and responding in the only appropriate way—with silent reverence and its companion hope.

LET US PRAY

You who are beyond what I can see
teach me to pray.
Help me to see your hand
and sense your presence wherever I look.
Let me approach the ordinary
and the commonplace with hope,
knowing that what I see
need never be all I get,
that mystery is there if only I will look
beyond what I can see.

You who are beyond mystery
hear my prayer.

3

To pray is to stand still
and to dwell upon a word.

—ABRAHAM JOSHUA HESCHEL

Only in that moment when we stand still long enough to confront a word, any word, when we do not flee from silence, do we begin to understand what Rabbi Heschel meant when he spoke of "knowing and not knowing." We understand and we don't understand. We see and we are blind. It is as though we had never heard the word before. And in the same breath we grasp, as though for the first time, what it means.

Only in that moment when our heart stands still do we experience in one and the same breath the mystery "of love and the inability to love." The one we love is never closer. Never farther away. Never so known. Never so unknowable.

In that moment we have a glimpse of the mystery of prayer—what prayer is and what it can be. In that moment a word, any word, opens into the wordless. We go to the core of our own stillness, our own quiet, where alone in the face of mystery we "address ourselves to him who is beyond the mystery." We pray.

It is a long distance from thinking of prayer as a stream of words, a long distance from "doing something."

Standing still is not easy for us.

LET US PRAY

You who are beyond mystery

hear my prayer.

Let my heart stand still long enough

to hear even a single word.

Let me follow it into stillness,

into that wordless core of silence

where you await me.

Where without words,

I can pray.

4

To become aware of the ineffable
is to part company with words.

—ABRAHAM JOSHUA HESCHEL

As long as we have a word for it, we feel relatively secure.

But in our spiritual journey, the rabbi reminds us, however persistently we pursue words, hoping to capture the ineffable, the more words recede. The more our security dissolves.

Where does this leave the God seeker who must part company with words if he is to discover a God who is beyond words? Where does it leave the searcher after the ineffable? Where does it leave those of us who are tempted more often than we care to admit to look for a caring God who will be for us a security blanket?

It leaves us, says the rabbi, free of the "illusion of total intelligibility," free of "the foolishness of ultimate self-reliance."

It leaves us free to pray, free to address ourselves to him who is beyond the mystery of knowing and not knowing, beyond our categories of knowable and unknowable, beyond speech and silence.

It leaves us free. Wordless, insecure, we are now free to live and pray full of wonder and radical amazement.

LET US PRAY

How do I pray to you
who are beyond the mystery of knowing
and not knowing,
beyond what is knowable and unknowable,
beyond speech and silence,
beyond the only words I know,
beyond the "prayers" I can say,
beyond the prayers I trust.
Set me free
so that, if just for this night,
I can pray to you,
not with words,
but with wonder and amazement.

5

The beginning of our happiness lies in the understanding that life without wonder is not worth living.

—ABRAHAM JOSHUA HESCHEL

The rabbi might have written: "Life without hope is not worth living."

Without wonder, without hope, we are forever walking through a landscape drained of color and promise. And God.

Without wonder, without hope we are condemned to live on the thin deceptive surface of our lives. We miss the miracle of what already is. But most of all we miss what could be, what is meant to be.

Without wonder, without hope we end up dragging our tails through too many endless days. We go to bed too many nights thinking that if this is all there is to life, it is not worth the price it extracts.

Without wonder, without hope we can live only half a life, a life that is only half worth living—a life confined to the outer wrappings of a world filled with mystery and the presence of God.

Wonder—hope—is not a fanciful option on our spiritual journey. It is the beginning, as the rabbi forcibly reminds us, of our happiness. It is the beginning of a life lived with miracles.

LET US PRAY

You who are beyond mystery
hear my prayer.
Let wonder loose in my soul.
Let hope begin.
Unwrap the mystery of your presence
for without it, without you,
I am living half a life.
Without wonder,
without hope
my life
is not, will not be
worth living.

The Present

JULIAN OF NORWICH

On one occasion the Lord told me:
"Everything will be all right."
It is as though he were telling us:
"live now in trust and faith,
and in the end
you will find fullness and joy."

He wishes us to know this
so that we can surrender our spirit
peacefully into his love,
and ignore every disturbance
that threatens our true rejoicing in God.

—JULIAN OF NORWICH

The Present

We live a life that cries out for healing in a world that keeps our wounds open. All is not well with us. "But all," Julian wrote over six centuries ago, "will be well."

At first blush such a promise sounds outrageously naive. It smacks of baby-talk, trivializing our pain into a boo-boo that can be kissed away, into one more slice of pie in the sky. It strikes us as uncannily close to hoping that life will go away.

The promise, however, is not that life will go away, that new wounds will never appear, that all will be healed. *The promise is that our wounds will lose their power to cripple us, their power to leave us feeling hopeless.*

Without hope we will spend our days obsessed by our failures, paralyzed by "what ails us," blind to what might be, confident that nothing will ever change, nothing will ever be better.

Most important it will put an end to our spiritual journey before it can get started. After all: why start on a journey that is going nowhere?

The promise that "all will be well" gives us permission to hope. We can "surrender our spirit peacefully into his love, and ignore every disturbance." We can, all evidence to the contrary, begin our spiritual journey and continue on our way.

It is not a question of putting off that journey until we are healed, but as Julian says, of living now "in trust and faith"—ignoring every disturbance that might threaten our true rejoicing in God.

It is a question of living *now*, trusting *now*, ignoring *now* anything that stands between us and the God who is the object of our hope.

Julian of Norwich
(1342-1420)

No one is certain exactly when she was born or when she died. No one in fact can be certain of her name. We do know that she lived in a kind of solitude in a cell attached to the Church of St. Edmund and St. Julian in Norwich, East Anglia, and that before her death she had gained a reputation for sanctity that attracted visitors from all over Europe.

What is not in doubt is the extraordinary experiences and spiritual wisdom she captured and left behind in a work sometimes called *Showings*, at other times *Revelations of Divine Love*. It is a timeless work that has remained century after century, and to this day, a powerful source of contemporary spirituality. For centuries she has been not only a timeless spiritual resource but a timely one.

What could be more timeless and timely than her going beyond traditional patriarchal notions of God to add the dimension of motherhood? There is something very contemporary, too, in her suspicion of traditional Christianity's obsession with sin. Even as she confesses her own weakness she insists that "all will be well."

She replaces a frequently inherited notion of God as tyrant with an image of a courteous lord who respects our humanity. In fact she created a whole language of words and images to convey her unique and sensitive vision of our life with God. We are comfortable with her sense of joy that too often we look for without finding in the works of the great mystics and spiritual masters.

Her independence and sensitivity break through any images we may have stored up for categorizing medieval nuns and their spirituality and help to explain why at the beginning of a new millennium she remains one of the most popular and influential of all spiritual writers. And we are intrigued that her book—the oldest work in English by a woman—is still in print and still sought out by those who are looking for wisdom with which to live in the twenty-first century.

There remains something very "now" about Julian of Norwich—whatever her name, whatever her dates.

I

It lasts now and forever because God loves it.

—JULIAN OF NORWICH

"God showed me," Julian wrote, "a little thing, no bigger than a hazelnut. And God said to me: 'It is all of creation.'"

Here was something so small, so fragile, that Julian was amazed that it did not disintegrate into nothingness.

"It exists," God told Julian, "because I love it."

"You exist because I love you."

It is a love that is not a matter of the heart, but our very existence.

In God's silent love we find hope, we are able to recognize, accept, and embrace our own fragility and finitude, our life at the edge of nothingness, our life sustained by a love we will never understand, that can never be returned.

We and our world, all of creation, may teeter on the edge of nothingness, but we are loved and so we exist.

LET US PRAY

Here on the edge of the night,

before I surrender my day

to the silent emptiness

of the dark,

I need to hear

that you love me.

I need to hear again your promise.

I need to hope in you.

Hear my prayer.

2

Our life in this world consists of a wondrous mixture of good and bad.

—JULIAN OF NORWICH

A world that we could write off as utterly bad or a world that we could presume as utterly good would be easier for us to live in than a world that is a wondrous mix of good and bad.

An utterly bad life or an utterly good life is something we could accept. But we are neither saints nor sinners, but like the world a wondrous mixture of good and bad.

We are not at all at ease rooting our hopes in such ambiguity. Perhaps this is why we so often subvert the spiritual journey into a search for security and certainty, for a definable God who delivers a definable life in a definable world.

We have a taste for certainties, securities. We want God to be about certainty, but she is the opposite. She is about ambiguity. To have certainty we would have to capture God in our words, our definitions, our categories. We would have to nail her down to what we can absorb and control.

God unnerves us. Our humanity upsets us.

"What a marvelous confusion," Julian wrote. "And it continues through our life. We never succumb to the pain and woe but always hope for another glimpse of his presence."

LET US PRAY

As this night begins
I glimpse your presence.
You are here
but always just beyond my fingertips,
just beyond my imaginings.
I know that you are here,
but as much as I desire to,
I cannot see your face,
I cannot capture you with my words,
but only with my hope.
Stay with me through this night.

3

He wishes us to know this so that our spirits
might be surrendered peacefully into his love.

—JULIAN OF NORWICH

We don't go peacefully into the hands of God.

Instead we struggle to prove our worthiness, our love for
God. It is as though we have to convince God that we are
lovable and loving, as though promises or not, all will not
end well unless we take charge.

"Before God created us," Julian wrote, "God loved us.
And that love never diminishes or ever shall." God wants
nothing more from us than our surrender to that love, letting him break through our self-centered conviction that
we need to be in control, that all need be well before we
are loved.

This is all he wishes us to know. It seems so little, but in
the end it may be the hardest truth of all to accept.

All will be well because it is not up to us.

LET US PRAY

Here as this night begins, I need to let go
to surrender my soul peacefully into your care,
knowing that even before you created me,
you loved me.
Your love has never diminished
nor ever shall.
Even so, it is hard for me
to go peacefully into this night.
It is hard for me to surrender.
You will have to take me
as I am.

4

Not only does he concern himself
with great and noble things,
but equally with small and simple things.

—JULIAN OF NORWICH

Long before we were being advised not to sweat the small stuff because it's all small stuff, Julian was celebrating its importance.

It's not just that God is every bit as present and available in "small and simple things" as he is in the events that make the headlines. It's that size doesn't matter. Nothing in life is small stuff. Or big stuff.

God doesn't know big. God doesn't know small. These are our categories. For God everything just is. And God cares about it because it is. Nothing else about it matters, because there is nothing else.

This is just one more example of how a God-driven spirituality requires us to leave behind the categories that we have used all our lives to make sense. Quantity—like other categories—is irrelevant because there is nothing of importance that can be measured by its standards. Everywhere he looks God sees only this—the immeasurable beauty of his creation. The fact that we are.

LET US PRAY

In all the "small" things of this day

you were there.

In all the "big" things,

you were there.

But none of them are important now.

None of them need follow me into the night.

You are here,

and that is all

I need to know,

all I need to bring with me.

5

God dwells within us—
We dwell within God.

—JULIAN OF NORWICH

"Our soul," Julian wrote, "is made to be God's resting place."

A place where God feels at home.

"And our soul is made to rest in God."

A place where we feel at home.

But the fact is that we are at best restless believers who are not totally at home either in God or in our souls. There's too much about the God that we carry around that makes us uneasy. There is too much about ourselves that leaves us unsatisfied.

If I am not at ease with myself, we think, how could God find his ease with me?

The answer is that however ill at ease we are with our soul, God feels right at home. We are his creation. God sees us as we are, and sees that "it is good."

We are the ones with the problem.

LET US PRAY

Now I lay down to rest
I pray you Lord:
be at ease with me,
with all that I am not,
with all I might be,
and let me at last
be at ease with you.
Comfortable with your love.
And loving as best I can,
lest I die before I wake,
having never loved you
as best I could.

This-Worldliness

DIETRICH BONHOEFFER

It is only by living completely in this world
that one learns to have hope.
One must completely abandon any attempt
to make something of oneself,
whether it be a saint, or a converted sinner,
or a churchman (a so-called priestly type!),
a righteous man or an unrighteous one,
a sick man or a healthy one.

By this-worldliness I mean
living unreservedly in life's duties
and problems,
successes and failures,
experiences and perplexities.
In so doing we throw ourselves completely
into the arms of God,
taking seriously, not our own sufferings,
but those of God in the world.

—DIETRICH BONHOEFFER

This-Worldliness

If ever the silence of God was more devastating, if ever there seemed to be fewer grounds for hope, it was the Holocaust years in which Bonhoeffer lived, prayed, preached, and died.

In such a climate "other-worldliness" is always an ongoing temptation. But Bonhoeffer recognized it for what it is: an illusionary and seductive escape to what does not exist. Real spirituality is lived out in a real world.

"This-world" spirituality—and this includes heroic sanctity—is always in and of this troubled, chaotic world, in and of its calendar, in and of its geography and its politics. What is easily and frequently forgotten is that it is also always in and of our troubled, chaotic human nature.

"By this worldliness," Bonhoeffer wrote to his friend, "I mean living unreservedly in life's duties, problems, successes and failures, experiences and perplexities."

Words like "certainty" and "security" are missing from his definition. The luxury of 20/20 hindsight is not guaranteed, not even provided. Hope does not come equipped with infallibility or even historical and political insight. God remains silent.

"This-worldly" spirituality is, therefore, almost inevitably a conflicted, ambiguous, half-blind version of our humanity and the world in which we are destined to live and make our act of hope and live out its consequences. That we believe in God does not mean that we automatically see what God sees, or even what God wants us to see.

Hope is not an exit pass out of our personal, family, civic, and religious history. It is just a way of living in what is and changing what we can to the extent that we can at whatever cost it exacts.

This might not have to be said if it were not for two things that dog western spirituality.

Our spiritual roots are in the desert and the monastery. As a result we choose, as often as not, our spiritual guidelines and heroes from the practices and ranks of the isolated and the secluded.

And second: we are bedeviled with a passion for perfection rather than humanity in our heroes. Absolute virtue, however, is a bad fit for our finitude. We are ill prepared to canonize ambiguity and conflict, blindness and deafness not just to the voice of God but to the voice of a demanding historic moment in and through which God speaks.

Given half a chance we are inclined to give the nod to the other-worldly. But from time to time we are forced to pay attention to someone like Dietrich Bonhoeffer, whose spiritual journey is, in hindsight, riddled with ambiguity.

Dietrich Bonhoeffer
(1906-1945)

Dietrich Bonhoeffer, Lutheran pastor and theologian, went to the gallows in a Nazi prison, charged not with being a Christian but with plotting the overthrow of Hitler—a political crime. For some—Christians mostly—he remains a martyr at a time of his own church's widespread complicity with Nazism. For others, Jews mostly, Bonhoeffer's death was just one final act of patriotism and institutional loyalty—the case of a man who died without finally grasping or responding to the role of the churches in the horror of the Holocaust.

He was a complex, conflicted scholar, pastor, and political activist in a complex, conflicted time. What is certain is that the times became his spiritual director, framing the challenges to his soul and pulling him step by torturous step into engagement with situations and questions that his training and loyalties had never prepared him to face, that his church had in fact over centuries helped to create. He was required, as one writer has summarized his situation, "to articulate a theology that truly confronted his times—and to do so without benefit of hindsight, but during the Third Reich itself."

"Life's duties, problems, successes and failures, experiences and perplexities" pulled him as they do us inevitably and critically into a world where there is no textbook, a world that we must confront without benefit of hindsight.

It is this lack of comfortable, reassuring hindsight that is the chief characteristic of a "this-worldly" spiritual journey. It is in fact for many of us only in retrospect that we begin to identify the questions that should have shaped our spiritual journey.

Our spiritual task is to "stand firm" in the midst of the unknown and unknowable. Who stands firm is he whose "final standard is not his reason, his principles, his virtue, but (he) who is ready to sacrifice all these, when in faith and sole allegiance to God he is called to obedient and responsible action: the person whose life will be nothing but an answer to God's question and call."

"Don't just stand there," he is saying, "do something, do what you must do." But remember that for Dietrich Bonhoeffer this insight came only in the shadow of the scaffold. We are not likely to improve on his record.

I

It is only by living completely in this world that one learns to have faith.

—DIETRICH BONHOEFFER

In 1939 Dietrich Bonhoeffer, for the second time, was visiting the United States and specifically New York's Union Theological Seminary. His American friends were certain that if he returned to Germany, prison was the best he could expect. With the courage he had already displayed, he had nothing to prove. He could, without embarrassment, join theologians Paul Tillich and Karl Barth in American exile.

He returned to his homeland without ever really explaining why except to tell a friend, Reinhold Niebuhr, that he felt that if he were not part of the struggle he would not be credible when it came time to rebuild. Being part of the struggle came to mean getting his hands dirty in political structures directed at the overthrow of Hitler, eventual imprisonment, and finally execution just days before Hitler's suicide.

In one of his last letters he would reject "the shallow and banal this-worldliness of the enlightened, the busy, the comfortable" to embrace a this-worldliness "characterized by discipline and the constant knowledge of death and resurrection."

No one could say that he did not live completely in this world.

No one could question the hope that sustained him there.

LET US PRAY

As this day ends
remind me,
lest I forget,
that this world
is a place of grace
for those who choose
to find you here.

But I must choose.

2

Cheap grace means grace sold on the market like cheap Jack's wares.

—DIETRICH BONHOEFFER

Cheap grace is Bonhoeffer's description of virtue that costs nothing.

It is how he names our coming to terms with evil, of learning to live with it at the least cost to ourselves, without regard for the cost to others. And all with the appearance of virtue.

It is a way of virtue forged in Nazi Germany as Jews, gays, and gypsies were being slaughtered even as a state religion debated whether non-Aryans could be, should be ordained.

It is a way of living that is alive and well wherever believers and the institutions of belief come to terms with evil for the sake of comfort and power.

Aversion to risk was and is its theology. Deafness to the pain of others was and is its armor. Silence was and is its native tongue.

But grace is not cheap. It is costly. It demands that we pay the price of risk, that we open our ears, that we speak when silence would cost us nothing.

LET US PRAY

Let not the silence of this night
cover over the voices
of this day.
Let not the darkness
hide the faces
of those in need.

Let me not
be a silent witness
to the evil
that keeps our world in pain.

Let not my silence
destroy me.
And others.

3

Grace is costly because it costs
a man his life.
And it is grace because it gives
a man the only true life.

—DIETRICH BONHOEFFER

Cheap grace has a lot in common with junk food. It's convenient, it tastes good, it looks like the real thing, but its capacity to nourish is near zero. Costly grace can be very inconvenient and unappetizing, but it exacts a high price. It is life-giving.

Bonhoeffer's life defined the difference.

Cheap grace is plumping for justice at an academic tea while safely surrounded by sympathetic friends. Costly grace is pursuing that same concern for justice all the way to a jail cell.

Bonhoeffer chose costly grace and over half a century later his jail cell is still generating life. The choice, of course, need not be this dramatic and seldom is.

What is really at stake is an everyday, undramatic attitude that somehow we can build a cost-free spiritual life. But you get what you pay for. And true life has never come cheap. Ask Bonhoeffer.

LET US PRAY

My soul
could starve to death
on a diet of the cheap grace
I seem to prefer.

I choose silence
when only words will do.
I choose words
when only deeds will do.
I choose the easiest
when only the difficult will do.

Let me choose your way
before my soul dies of hunger.

4

We have been silent witnesses of evil deeds.

—DIETRICH BONHOEFFER

The high spiritual drama of believers in a Nazi state wrote large the quiet dramas of believers on any given day, in any given state. Our drama in our state.

We are silent witnesses of evil deeds. We sacrifice the poor, the homeless, the hungry, the prisoners, the "outsiders" to an economic theory posing as a moral code.

"The market will care for them. Blessed are the market-makers."

But our silence like the silence of believers in Hitler's Germany and the world's churches has not brought us peace. It can't. It has not built for our souls a hiding place. It can't.

Instead it has made us victims of our own equivocations. We have learned to turn a blind eye. We have learned to lie to ourselves with rationalizations that separate us from what is real, from the convictions that we have counted on to hold us together.

"Will our inward power of resistance be strong enough," Bonhoeffer wondered, "and our honesty with ourselves be remorseless enough, for us to find our way back to simplicity and straightforwardness?" We wonder.

LET US PRAY

This is not the time
or the place
to close my eyes.

This is not the time
or the place
to deafen my ears.

Here in the dark
let my heart
see and hear
the truth.

5

Freedom comes only through deeds,
not through thoughts taking wing.

—DIETRICH BONHOEFFER

There is a thin line between spirituality and self-obsession. And because it seems that we can regularly cross it with hardly a thought, we need to be reminded that spirituality like freedom "comes only through deeds—not through thoughts taking wing."

Climbing into some comfortable corner of our soul and dreaming pious dreams of God's love is not spirituality, it is ego-tripping.

We are compelled, as Andrew Harvey reminds us, to pass that love on to others "and not in a purely emotional or even spiritual way either, but in a dynamically practical way, a way that demands of all of us a stark look at real conditions and their remedies."

The world is not to be escaped or enveloped in clouds of wishful thinking; it is to be confronted—at whatever cost.

"Daring to do what is right," Bonhoeffer urged us in the final days of his life, "not what fancy may tell you . . . go out to the storm and the action."

LET US PRAY

I do not easily
give up my comfort
or my need
for a life without cost.

I prefer cheap grace
to costly deeds
and an untroubled heart
to a heart open to the world.

I prefer easy peace
To entering the storm.

But you know that.

Others

DOROTHY DAY

True love is delicate and kind,
full of gentle perception and understanding,
full of beauty and grace,
full of joy unutterable.

There should be some flavor of this
in all our love for others.
We are all one.
We are one flesh in the Mystical Body,
as man and woman are said to be
one flesh in marriage.
With such a love
one would see all things new;
we would begin to see people
as they really are,
as God sees them.

—DOROTHY DAY

Others

Robert Ellsberg got it exactly right when he wrote of Dorothy Day: "It was not what Dorothy Day wrote that was extraordinary, nor even what she believed, but the fact that there was absolutely no distinction between what she believed, what she wrote, and the manner in which she lived."

That same insight put the finger on the heart of all true spirituality—the continuity and inseparability of conviction and action. It's what made us nervous in her presence (and I for one was nervous) and frightened by our own disjointed life. It never occurred to her, as it so often does to us, that spirituality could begin and end in the protective, seductive privacy of the soul.

Because our spiritual search sends us deeply within our soul there is a great temptation to stay there, to spend our days wrapped in the comfort of isolation from the world that is hungry, homeless, naked, and imprisoned. We are too easily caught up in our inner struggle with a silent god. But only when we turn outward to the others do we find and live out our hope.

There can be and often is a thin line between spirituality and narcissism. But perhaps because Dorothy Day's call to faith began with and remained rooted in and inseparable from her social consciousness her faith never turned inward. There were for her always the "others" and those "others" were always the poor—the poor who are always with us and with whom she lived out her life and her hope.

Things don't change much. In 1943 she could write: "We meet good people who are under the delusion that there is little poverty in the United States, that we are all enjoying a high standard of living." Sound familiar? And when presented with the facts they blame the poor. "It must be their own fault. They are shiftless. Anyone can get a job these days."

There is timelessness to the problem and to the response of Dorothy Day. The poor must be served because their need cries out to us. Even if we don't know whether God is real or present, we serve them and in that service catch a glimmer of hope that maybe God is there.

We may in time, under her tutelage, come to see God in the poor and see the poor as God sees them, his children, our brothers and sisters. But in the meantime, her teaching, her life is clear.

We can run from the streets but we cannot hide.

The "others" we have always with us.

Dorothy Day
(1897-1980)

For some years now there has been an anecdote circulating that cuts to the heart of Dorothy Day's impact. A very conservative Catholic archbishop far from Dorothy Day in the politics of poverty and peace was said to regularly send the Catholic Worker a check for $25,000. When asked why, he answered: "Because there is an outside chance that she's a saint."

Cardinal O'Connor admitted that Dorothy Day made him "worry." The fact is that Dorothy Day's life made us all worry, made us all uneasy with our easy believing. She still does. We have the reluctant suspicion, not that she was a saint, but just someone who got it right, that what she believed and how she lived was and is the way it's supposed to be—that we are kidding ourselves about what it means to profess belief in God.

But it took a while for her to get it right. Before there were Catholic Worker hospitality houses for the poor, before there was shared tenement poverty, before there was jail time for opposition to war and support of farm-workers rights, there was a woman who wrote for communist newspapers as well as screenplays (albeit briefly) for the establishment. Before she became a model and mentor for several generations of committed young people, there was a woman who was still there at "closing time," who spent years trying to stop smoking, and who had a variety of lovers and two babies, one of which she aborted.

The continuity of her life was an ever-increasing sympathy for the truly poor, the street poor, and a passionate conviction that not only was there something that could and must be done, but that she was called to do that something.

She was in the same breath convinced that you could not help the poor without choosing and sharing their poverty. She wasn't talking uptown poverty. The poverty she chose to share voluntarily, which she never got used to, was a poverty of "cockroaches, bedbugs, body lice, fleas, rats and such like vermin that goes with poverty." It was not a poverty to be celebrated or romanticized but a poverty to be fought, a poverty that should rack the nations and their believers.

She knew too that such a struggle could not be made alone. In the beginning there was "movement" support. In the end there was her common hope and her community of workers, all poor, some voluntarily so.

Hers was the kind of life, the kind of hope designed to "worry" our conscience, to undermine what we too often have come to think of as spirituality, the kind of life that challenges the silence of our souls and of our neighborhood.

I

Life itself is a haphazard, untidy, messy affair.

—DOROTHY DAY

Our search for God and our service to others will never be conducted in a neat world. Life will never submit to our good intentions, will never fall in line, will never stand still long enough to do our bidding.

Life will never cease to be a messy affair and our spiritual journey will never be reduced to a tidying-up operation. God and the others don't wait to enter our life until we have put it all in order.

Our journey—Dorothy Day would call it our *pilgrimage*—is about finding God and serving others in the midst of the mess. And it is no less messy in the neatest suburb than on New York's Lower East Side where the Catholic Workers still welcome anyone in need.

The messiest place of all will be our own soul, our own life, which despite our best efforts will insist on remaining human. And it is into this mess, this confusion, that God and others will invite themselves.

"Oh, the house is such a mess! But you are just in time for dinner!"

"Make yourself at home!"

LET US PRAY

As this night closes in
welcome, Lord, to this mess.
It's my mess.
It's who I am.
It's all I have
to offer you.
Take it, Lord,
for what it is,
for who I am.

2

The work is as basic as bread.

—DOROTHY DAY

As practiced by Dorothy Day, serving others can seem overwhelming, demanding far more from us than we are prepared to give. It has taken a lifetime to put and keep a roof over our family, and we are not prepared to abandon it for life with the "street people."

But dramatizing her message to the point where it becomes for most of us an impossibility is a sure-fire way of excusing us from what in fact we can and should do. Because we can't do everything, we are not excused from doing something. Doing nothing is not an option.

Our obligation "is as basic as bread." Putting bread where there is no bread. There is nothing exotic or mysterious or impossible about it. As she is fond of reminding us: it's no more complicated than that unused coat in the closet. It belongs on the back of someone else, someone who needs it.

The problem for many of us is remembering in an age of our own abundance that we have two coats and two loaves and that there is someone, millions of someones, without a coat or a single loaf.

We can do something.

LET US PRAY

As this night closes in
I am not hungry,
I am not cold,
I am not homeless,
but there are those who are.
Sleep will not come easily to them.
Nor should I rest
as long as they go hungry,
as long as they are cold,
as long as they are homeless.

This coming day
let me share with them
my daily bread.

We are walking in love and love is all that we want.

—DOROTHY DAY

Love may be all *we* want, but for a single mother with two kids another bedroom would be nice.

Love may be all *we* want but a disarmed world would be nice.

"It is hard to love," Dorothy Day wrote, "from the human standpoint and from the divine standpoint, in a two room apartment." Or in a country pulled apart by religious and ethnic violence.

Her mission, the core of her spirituality, was to build a world in which it would be easier to lead a good life. In which it would be easier to walk in love.

She made her contribution to that world by reaching out to those in need, deserving, undeserving, grateful or not, by saying "no" to war, not just with words but by putting her body in its way, by never separating the spirit from the world in which the spirit lives.

For her, as in the end for all of us, the service of others is not an overflow of a "spiritual" life, but its origin and driving force.

Only when we walk with others are we walking in love.

LET US PRAY

As this night closes in
I yearn for a world
where it would be easier for me
to lead the good life
that I only dream of.
But the price is so high.
I would have to see all things new;
I would have to see all the others
as they really are,
as you see them.
Open my eyes to them.
Open my heart.
Only then can I hope
to walk in love.

4

Be mutually careful one for another.

—DOROTHY DAY

It is as a New Year's resolution that Dorothy Day prays that we might "be mutually careful one for another."

It is a modest prayer—a modest hope, a modest goal as a new year begins. But it recognizes how fragile we are, how vulnerable even the most street-toughened can be, how delicate the thickest-skinned soul still is.

We, all of us, need to be handled with care, and to "be mutually careful one for another." Caring for one another, being gentle with one another, making life easier for one another is no little thing.

For Dorothy Day it was a vocation, a lifelong commitment. It was the spiritual work of mercy that accompanied and undergirded her caring for the street's physically needy. For her it meant being especially "careful" of those who had long since lost hope: the angry, the disappointed, the defeated, those whom she welcomed off the streets with her offer of unquestioning hospitality.

"True love"—*true caring*, she might have said—"is delicate and kind, full of gentle perception and understanding, full of beauty and grace, full of joy unutterable."

LET US PRAY

As this night closes in

let me resolve

to be more

mutually careful for others.

It is not much,

but it is the least

that I can do for another.

We are all fragile.

"Handle with care."

5

We will always get what we need.

—DOROTHY DAY

Just about everything about Dorothy Day flew in the face of common sense—which is just about as good a definition of her spirituality as any we might formulate. And the scariest.

You don't live your life with "no thought for what you shall eat or drink," but Dorothy Day did.

Everybody knows that you don't set out to provide food and shelter for thousands without short and long-term business plans. You put together a well-heeled board of directors to worry about endowments and liability insurance. You don't let things "just happen." That would be crazy. Everybody knows that. It's just common sense.

Dorothy Day flew in the face of that common sense. She opened her doors and the poor came. They were sheltered and they were fed.

Spirituality, she taught us, always flies in the face of marketplace logic. God opens doors and we come. It doesn't make sense to believe in God, to live with his silence. But we do.

LET US PRAY

As this night closes in

I worry about tomorrow,

what I shall eat,

what I shall put on.

You know, Lord, that

I have need of these things.

But tomorrow may never come.

Be with me now.

The
Commonplace

MEISTER ECKHART

Some people prefer solitude.
They say their peace of mind
depends on this.
Others say they would be
better off in church.
If you do well, you do well wherever you are.
If you fail, you fail wherever you are.
Your surroundings don't matter.

God is with you everywhere—
in the marketplace
as much as in seclusion or in the church.

If you look for nothing but God,
nothing or no one can disturb you.
God is not distracted
by a multitude of things.
Nor can we be.

—MEISTER ECKHART

The Commonplace

The most effective way to scuttle a spiritual life is to put it out of reach.

Reserve prayer for the specialists, silence for the monks, spirituality for the leisure class, those assured of their daily bread. Exclude those who pay rent, sweat out the pay period, work two jobs and change diapers, and scramble for their daily bread.

There has always been a feeling that for a spiritual life you needed to be a certain kind of person, someone with a taste and talent for things spiritual. You also needed the right setting.

Six hundred years ago Eckhart noted that "some people prefer solitude. They say their peace of mind depends on this. Others say they would be better off in church."

"But it doesn't matter where you are," he wrote. "If you do well you do well wherever you are. If you fail you fail wherever you are. Your surroundings don't matter."

God is with you everywhere—
in the marketplace
as much as in seclusion or in the church.

The point of this, however, is not just a plea for class-less prayer. It is a reminder that the heart of western spirituality is "the practice of the presence of God."

Perhaps because over the centuries it has been closely associated with Brother Lawrence, the lay brother who worked out his spirituality in a kitchen and at his shoe-maker's bench, this practice seems too simple, too obvious, too homely for the spiritually ambitious.

But it was not too simple for Eckhart the scholar and mystic.

More than three centuries separate the two holy men, but their spirituality took root in the same commonplace truth.

They shared a conviction that God, however silent, is never out of reach.

Meister Eckhart
(1260-c. 1328)

Meister Eckhart has had two lifetimes. The first stretched from his birth to his death, not quite seventy years later. For a few decades more there were followers to keep his memory alive. The second began more than five centuries later and is only now beginning to flourish.

The first lifetime was a time of scholarship and responsible work with a persistent subtext of controversy that remains to this day. The scholarship was highly speculative, subtle, innovative, and provocative. His writings about God were balanced on highly nuanced distinctions that more often than not failed to satisfy those charged with protecting theological orthodoxy. He wrote in the tradition of "negative" theology. To use a simplistic example he might have said that "God is not good," meaning that God is not good in any way that we can understand. But many of his listeners heard ideas bordering on heresy.

He was constantly defending himself even as his religious superiors overlooked the criticism and appointed him to increasingly responsible roles in the governance and education of his fellow Dominican friars. He would in the end "recant" any possible errors in his teaching and his followers would be told to exercise prudence in what they believed and taught.

In the long run, however, it would not be his speculative theology that would bring him back to life. In the late twentieth century he would become an increasingly popular spiritual master, joining the ranks of the great mystics sought out by those in search of a deeper spiritual life. What we have of his spiritual writings, mostly sermons, displays a simple straightforwardness that is in sharp contrast to the complexity of his theological speculations.

He wrote not for a spiritual elite but for the common folk. He wrote not in the Latin of officialdom but in German, the language of the people. But he was writing about the mystical path to God. The effect was often inflammatory. Richard Chilson puts it this way: "He brought mysticism to the masses and thus provoked concern among some of the hierarchy that his ideas, even if orthodox in themselves, might be misinterpreted."

In the internally directed spirituality of Eckhart what is important is not what we do, but where our heart is. Our task is to turn to God and be directed by him along a path unique to each of us. It may point us to a monastic cell, but it is just as likely that it will point us to the marketplace. What we must not forget is that spirituality does not end in the privacy of the soul but in the service of the poor.

"For Eckhart," as Chilson has written, "God and God alone is reality. Anything else is at best a means or at worse an obstacle." It is for anyone seeking a spiritual direction a message that is at once clear, accessible, and challenging. Discovered by whole new generations it has given Meister Eckhart a second life.

I

God isn't interested in what you do.

—MEISTER ECKHART

When Meister Eckhart tells us that God isn't interested in what we do, he isn't playing cute. He is cutting to the heart of western spirituality.

Spirituality is not about doing, it is about being. It is about recognizing and accepting the fundamental truth that God isn't interested in what we do because nothing we can do can affect his love for us. That love never changes. That love is never earned. That love is never lost.

But that love is never an excuse to do nothing, to watch the poor go hungry and homeless while we sit by, basking in divine favor. It is rather to understand that to be possessed by God's love is to be driven to demonstrate that love by loving others. It is not as a way of gaining God's favor. That can't be done. It's a given. We don't qualify for it. It's not a reward to be withdrawn at any moment, even in that moment when we ignore the needs of the least of our brothers and sisters.

It's not an easy message for "achievers." Outright gifts make us uneasy. We prefer to think that we have done something to qualify for this divine largesse.

"Remember me God, I'm the one who. . . ."

LET US PRAY

As this night closes in

I need not remind you

of who I am

or what I have done.

I am the one who needs to remember.

I am someone you love.

That is enough.

2

Nobody at any time is cut off from God.

—MEISTER ECKHART

Childhood religion has left many of us with the idea that sin, bad stuff—call it what you will—cuts us off from God.

It can't be done.

"Whether you go away or return," Eckhart writes, "God never leaves you. God is always present." Even if we systematically try to write him out of our lives, running around closing doors, it won't work. Even if "God cannot enter your life, he is no farther away than the door." Even when we close our ears to his knock.

Don't mistake the silence of God for a mere passive presence. It is not a case of God standing by on some street corner of our life waiting to be recognized and acknowledged.

His presence is an active presence. He is actively, positively, at work in our lives even when we wish he weren't, even when our childhood religion tells us that we have driven him out.

Nobody at any time is cut off from God. Nobody. Ever.

Whether we feel it or not.

LET US PRAY

As this night closes in
let me enter into its silence and darkness
knowing that you are here.
Not as a judge,
not as an intruder,
but as a lover.
Whether I feel your presence or not,
whether I think that given this day,
you should be here.

Nobody, not even me,
is ever cut off from you.
You never leave.
You are always here.
Remind me.

3

The light shines in the darkness, and in the darkness we become conscious of it.

—MEISTER ECKHART

To be "left in the dark" has become a metaphor for exclusion and deprivation. But in the world of the spirit it is a place of discovery.

The night sky is a spectacular reminder that it is only with the coming of darkness that we can see the starlight that was there all along. Until nightfall it gives way to the blinding light of the sun.

And like starlight, God's light "shines in the darkness, and in the darkness we become conscious of it."

There is no question that for many of us, even most of us, the night is a beautiful place, but we wouldn't want to live there. We would prefer a spiritual world lit always by a blazing sun that would clarify and illuminate every step of our journey. We can't wait for the dawn. But in the darkness and silence of the night, free of day's light, we become conscious of God's light. There is too much to see during the day. The daylight distracts us, blinds us even to the subtler light of the stars.

But here in the dark silence of the night we become aware of a presence that we might otherwise miss.

She prefers to "leave us" where we are more likely to see her.

LET US PRAY

As this night closes in
let me embrace its dark
and its silence.
Let me leave behind
the brightness and sounds
of the day just past.

The better to see you,
to let your light
shine in this darkness.
Let it light up the night.
Let it light up my life.

4

God is God of the present.

—MEISTER ECKHART

Perhaps it is because God is so frequently summed up in abstractions like omnipotence and ubiquity that we are inclined to think of God as an abstraction.

Eckhart cuts through our foggy piety with a simple statement: "God is God of the present." There is no point in seeking God in times past or in the future: God is here, God is now. We need not look somewhere else, at some other time. There is no point in searching out the right words, the right encompassing formula.

God is always in the present tense. It is never a case of "God loves us." It is always: "God is loving us now." Our life is lived in the present tense. It is not a case of "I love God." It is a case of "I am loving God now."

God is there where time and definitions collapse, where there is only now.

To acknowledge this present, this now, is a kind of rescue operation, a kind of holding operation, an attempt to keep God from being frozen into the words and images of our childhood or into harmless abstractions that keep her safely, undemandingly at arm's length.

A "God" who is the "God of the present"—of our present— does not easily go away, is not easily dissolved into a warm memory or a frightening future.

A "God of the present" is here, is to be reckoned with.

LET US PRAY

Now

as this night closes in,

I lay me down to sleep.

Now.

I pray the Lord

my soul to keep.

Now.

5

It is impossible to lose God.

—MEISTER ECKHART

The problem of course is identifying "being good" with "having God," and "being bad" with "losing God." But God is not to be "had" or "lost."

The God to whom we tie our hopes doesn't practice our childish petulance, triviality, inconsistency, and pettiness. "I'm not talking to you anymore!"

God's love—we have to repeat constantly to ourselves— is not a conditional love. It does not depend on what we do, but solely on the fact that we are.

This is hard for us to believe because we keep measuring God by our standards and by the standards of those who claim to speak for God.

We don't lose God but we too often lose ourselves when we restrict our vision of God to a God of our own making. Any God that we can conceive is a God that can slip away.

"You do not want your idea of God, but rather the reality of God," Eckhart writes. That God cannot be lost.

LET US PRAY

As this night closes in
let me end this day
knowing
that I cannot lose you,
that nothing I have done this day
changes the fact
that I am loved unconditionally
by you.

Let me enter the night
trusting in that love
and wake to a promise kept.
Your love will still be there.
You will still be there.

The Desert

CHARLES DE FOUCAULD

God calls all the souls he has created
to love him
with their whole being,
here and hereafter,
which means that he calls all of them
to holiness, to perfection,
to a close following of him,
an obedience to his will.
But he does not ask all souls
to show their love
by the same works,
to climb to heaven by the same ladder,
to achieve goodness
in the same way.

—CHARLES DE FOUCAULD

The Desert

When Charles de Foucauld moved step by step from self-indulgent years as a French military officer to a contemplative existence in the Algerian Sahara it was because he had determined for himself that the key to his spiritual growth would be an ever closer imitation of the Nazareth years of Jesus, the hidden years.

Imitation is not an unusual form of spirituality. Periodically, as Robert Ellsberg has pointed out, "seekers manage to reinvent the 'imitation of Christ' in a manner suited to the needs of their age." Others seek to walk in the shoes of the Buddha, Mohammed, or Abraham.

What made de Foucauld's imitation noteworthy in our times, however, was its intensity, its totality, its literalness. He was determined to leave behind the relative comfort of monastic life for the isolation and solitude of the desert where alone, he felt, he could live out his calling.

In this he was not the first seeker to be drawn by desert asceticism. As early as the third century men and women sought out the desert as a center for their spiritual journey. But de Foucauld sought out the desert not for its isolation and solitude. He was not "fleeing" anywhere, not escaping anything. He sought out the most isolated, least inhabited part of the Sahara to establish and celebrate the presence of God by establishing his own presence and accessibility, by imitating the silent presence of Jesus' Nazareth years.

In his own time, despite his deeply felt lack of followers, no one accepted his invitation to share his desert calling. It would not be until twenty years after his death that followers would appear to turn his vision into a religious community.

His legacy of a spirituality suitable for desert living would become a critical part of the spiritual landscape because for many, the world we live in has become a desert experience that knows no denominational, geographical, or temporal bounds. It is all the desert we need. We don't have to go anywhere looking for desert. We need only look around and within.

Charles de Foucauld
(1858-1916)

Viscount Charles-Eugene de Foucauld, his title and aristocratic roots long since left behind, was already forty-seven years old but a priest for only four years when in 1905 he first saw the Algerian village where he would fulfill his mission and spend the rest of his life.

Tamanrasset, a sun-baked mountain village (4600 feet above sea level), was home to only twenty or so Muslim families of Tuaregs, a semi-nomadic people known for their prowess in battle. It was what his heart desired, a place of almost total isolation (his nearest fellow priest hundreds of desert and mountain miles away) that offered him the spiritual Nazareth he had long sought. At the edge of the village he built a two-room stone cottage that he would later expand in a never-to-be-satisfied hope that others would join him in his ministry of silent presence. In time the Muslim villagers would recognize in him a *marabout*, holy man; but they would never embrace his religion. He in turn would call himself a "little brother of Jesus."

His journey to Tamanrasset did not, however, begin until his late twenties. Until then "Piggy Foucauld" was more distinguished for high living than for self-discipline. With a significant inheritance in his pocket, natural charm, and family connections, he managed to survive a track record of mischievous behavior to become a commissioned officer in the French army with a first assignment to Africa. Here began a fascination with the Algerian desert whose geography he would explore and write about and eventually embrace, and with the impressive Muslim faith of its natives that would lead him to a rethinking of his own religious roots. His exposure to Islam "and to the soul living always in God's presence helped me understand that there is something greater and more real than the pleasures of this world."

"As soon as I believed there was a God, I understood that I could not do anything but live for him. My religious vocation dates from the same moment as my faith."

It would be almost twenty more years (1905) before it would take its final shape at Tamanrasset. First he traveled to the Holy Land and became a monk in a Syrian Trappist monastery, only to discover that its austerity was not pure enough to satisfy his increasing spiritual hunger. In a Nazareth convent he lived as a janitor until under much urging he became a priest and began to formulate a dream of a religious community that would practice the spirituality of the Nazareth years, a rule of life that would find its solitary expression in Tamanrasset.

Eleven years later in a moment of exquisite symbolism the Tamanrasset experiment would end when, still alone, he was killed as a French sympathizer. Still another twenty years would pass before his dream of a religious community living his rule would be a reality that remains to this day.

Love consists not in feeling that we love,
but in wanting to love.

—CHARLES DE FOUCAULD

As often as not our spiritual journey falters not from a lack of will, but from a lack of imagination.

Charles de Foucauld will long be remembered for the solitude, the sacrifice, the single-mindedness of his life, the sweet irony of his death in Tamanrasset. But long before he felt the heat of its days and the chill of its nights de Foucauld knew what it was he wanted, what might be, what could be, what for him had to be.

He imagined his Nazareth into being. His imagination fueled his journey from "officer's quarters" to the cells of Tamanrasset.

It made it possible for him to walk in someone else's shoes.

It made it possible for him to walk in God's shoes.

Our own journey too often stops short because we are satisfied with what we can see, with what is familiar, with the comfort of our own shoes.

But our own journey cannot get underway until we surrender to our imagination. Only then can we release and build on the hope that is in us.

LET US PRAY

Let me journey into this night
walking in your shoes.
Let me surrender to its silence and its dark
imagining what might be.
I too need a Nazareth where I can grow
in silence and hope,
in wisdom and age
before God and humanity.
Take me there
if only in my imagination.
Loan me your shoes.

2

My God, if you exist, make your existence known to me.

—CHARLES DE FOUCAULD

Biographers describe a twenty-eight-year-old de Foucauld wandering the streets of Paris begging God to show his face, pleading with her to break her silence.

We know the need. We have been there, done that.

But despite our pleading, God has kept her face hidden, left her silence unbroken. If we have come to "know" his existence it is only because we have come to terms with the silence, come to bank on what we cannot see.

We have come to accept—however reluctantly—that if God is going to be a part of our life our only option is faith, a life lived without tangible assurances, without demonstrable certainties.

Despite our most earnest pleading, God is not going to surrender to our conditions. "If you show me your face, if you speak to me, I'll believe."

Faced with God's silence de Foucauld asked for advice from a confessor who told him in effect to stop looking for what could not be had. Just accept that when it comes to God, hope is unavoidable.

LET US PRAY

I know better,
but even so, for one quiet moment
as darkness overtakes my day,
I wish faith were not necessary.
I want to see your face
and hear your voice.
"My God, if you exist,
make your existence known to me."

Forgive my unbelief.
Forgive my need to catch sight of you
in the dark.

3

My religious vocation dates from the same
moment as my faith.

—CHARLES DE FOUCAULD

However often we speak of the silence and the dark
where an unseen and silent God is seen and heard, however much we treasure such space and seek it out, when
God happens in our life it is not an invitation to crawl into
his silence and darkness and hide there. God never issues
us an invitation to wrap ourselves in him, to use his presence as a protective coating designed to seal out life and
others.

There is no hiding. "Life" is what happens, as the T-shirt
has it, when we have other plans. "Others" are what happens when we try to become an island. God is not an exit
route from either. Rather, when we open our hearts to life
and others God happens in our lives.

For de Foucauld a religious vocation, a call, a reaching out
began in the same moment as his faith. The seed of
Tamanrasset began to take root. The moment we let God
in, the moment we acknowledge his presence, the whole
world follows.

This doesn't mean that we are called to become monks, to
find our own Tamanrasset. But we are called to life. We
are called to others.

Hope does not offer a substitute existence.

LET US PRAY

As this night begins,
I would, if I could,
keep you to myself.
I would hide in your presence
from all the aches and pains,
from all the silliness of this day
that still crowds around me.
But there is no hiding.
You are wherever life is.
You are wherever others are.
You belong to no one.

4

The life of Nazareth can be followed anywhere.

—CHARLES DE FOUCAULD

Then de Foucauld refined his advice. "Follow it," he said, "in the place where it is most helpful to your neighbors."

Helpful not to you, but to your neighbor.

For neighbors he chose a nomadic tribe of the Sahara. In the years after his death his followers lived in fraternities and worked side by side with their blue-collar and working-poor neighbors. For most of us it will not be a question of choosing our neighbors, but of serving the ones that life gives us.

In the process Nazareth will be where Nazareth will be—where we are. And God will be found and served where God is to be found and served—wherever we are.

The task is to take our eyes off ourselves and look out for our neighbors.

The task is to remind ourselves daily that spirituality in the long run is not about being "holy," but about being neighborly.

Obviously in the worst neighborhoods, not so obviously in the best neighborhoods.

And always in the desert.

LET US PRAY

Let me make room
in the silence and the dark
for something more
than my own
cares and concerns.
Let my neighbors in,
for without them
you are not here,
there is only me,
and I am not enough.

5

Real faith . . . strips the world of its mask
and reveals God in all things.

—CHARLES DE FOUCAULD

What can seem dry, lifeless, desolate, and without
promise—our life, our marriage, our job, our world, the
relentless ordinariness of our days—is waiting to be
recognized for what it is: God's everyday face, a land
waiting to flower, a place of opportunity.

But our temptation is to believe that God is not in the
sandy stretches but in the oases, that God *is* in fact an
oasis, a relief from the arid landscape of our lives rather
than a promise waiting to be kept, a beckoning presence
waiting to be unmasked.

It is a temptation that can send us chasing after every
mirage, every vague promise of escape from the desert.
We end up locating God not in the gritty reality of our
everyday world, but in rainbow illusions. We place our
hope not in what is, but in fantasy that forever retreats at
our approach, that remains forever somewhere over the
rainbow.

But our hope is in our desert home, however dry, lifeless,
desolate, and without promise our days may seem to be,
and in a desert hope that strips the world of its mask to
reveal God in all things.

LET US PRAY

As this day ends
I have no desire to close my eyes
to what is.
I have no desire
to escape
to what might be.

You are what is.
What else could I want
as this day ends?

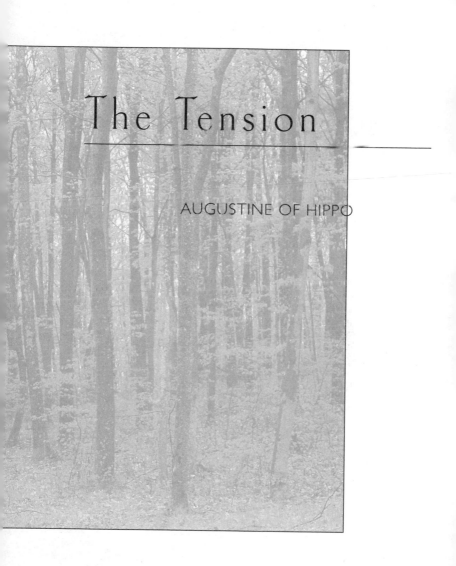

The Tension

AUGUSTINE OF HIPPO

Late have I loved you.
Beauty so ancient and so new,
late have I loved you!
You were within me
but I was seeking you outside.
In my ugliness
I plunged into the beauties you have made.
You were with me, but I was not with you.
The beauties I could see
kept me far from you,
yet if they had not been in you,
they would not have existed at all.
You called, you cried out,
you shattered my deafness;
you flashed,
you shone,
you scattered my blindness.
I was hungry and thirsty.
You touched me,
and I burned for your peace.

—AUGUSTINE OF HIPPO

The Tension

At the center of spirituality there is a tension that has been with us since the first creature tried to seek God without abandoning his creation. No spiritual teacher has felt this tension more profoundly and more personally than Augustine. No one has written about it with greater passion.

He knew well that the extravagant beauty of God's creation, the dazzling generosity of his gift can seem at times enough, more than enough to feed the hunger of our soul.

With such beauty all around us and within us, who needs God? With such beauty at our fingertips, in the air we breathe, in the passions we feel, who needs to seek after mystery, after what cannot be seen or touched or felt?

But he also knew well the pull of the creator and the temptation to abandon creation and deny its beauty in order to remove anything and everything that might come between him and beauty's creator.

Must we choose between the creator and his creation, between body and soul? Must we choose?

Augustine knew, as we must come to know, that choosing between creator and creation is not an option.

> *The beauties I could see kept me far from you,*
> *yet if they had not been in you,*
> *they would not have existed at all.*

We come to know and love all creation and ourselves because together we exist in God. Creature and creator are inseparable. We cannot love one without the other. Most important we cannot love ourselves apart from creation, apart from its, our creator.

Augustine of Hippo
(354-430)

Augustine lived and debated theology at a time when the spiritual tension between creator and creature, between flesh and spirit had become a crisis that was threatening to pull Christendom apart . . . and individual lives, including Augustine's.

There were the Manicheans who believed that the material world was the creation of the powers of evil and was therefore to be shunned. There were the Donatists who believed only the virtuous qualified for church membership. Church rites, the sacraments, were valid only when administered by the pure. And there were the Pelagians who taught that we inherit original virtue rather than original sin.

The debates raged not just among the scholars and churchmen, but in the public arena. Donatists could not make wills, sue, or hold office. And as formally convicted heretics they could be executed. It was the bloody height of an argument that has never gone away. Its insistent presence in our theology and our lives is a reminder of how stubborn is the struggle between body and soul, between creator and creation. That struggle is in a very real sense the story of Augustine.

For sixteen centuries now Augustine's spiritual autobiography, the *Confessions*, has been read as a timeless guide to self-understanding. It is the always contemporary story of a man caught up in a worldly life who undergoes a profound religious conversion—but not all that willingly. He puts it off as long as he can, making his story a textbook case of: "I want to be a saint, but not yet!"

But more important and helpful over the centuries has been Augustine's portrayal of conversion as a never-ending process, something that is never quite complete. It was an extraordinary admission in a world where conversion was more often than not pictured as "instant cure," as indeed it sometimes still is. It is never a question of creator or creation. We don't go to bed a struggling sinner and wake up a tranquil saint. The world doesn't go away. But neither does God.

Augustine was, and so in our best moments are we, "a *recovering* sinner, not a *former* sinner." Late we may come to our own conversion, but like Augustine we do come, however reluctant, however much a work in progress.

You would not be looking for me
if you had not already found me.

—AUGUSTINE OF HIPPO

"Journey" is at best a mischievous, even an unfortunate spiritual metaphor. It implies that wherever we are, God is somewhere else and must be tracked down. At best it presumes an absent God, at worst a fleeing God.

It is a metaphor that implies that God is found somewhere at the end of a process that begins without her. The God of "journey" becomes a treasure to be hunted, an evanescent pot of gold at the end of a spiritual rainbow, always just beyond our reach. The distance is never closing.

"Journey" is a red herring. We would not be starting that journey, as Augustine learned, if it were not already completed.

God is where we are. God is not a treasure hidden somewhere out there but a treasure to be discovered where we are, where God always is.

We would not be looking for God if we had not already found her. God is not at the end of a path. God is the path.

LET US PRAY

Even here
at the wordless end of a day
I need look no farther
than the dark and silence
of this night,
the silence of this place,
the hunger of my soul.
You are not somewhere else,
you are here.
You are here where I am.
I am where you are.
I need not look for you
for you have found me.

2

You touched me,
and I burned for your peace.

—AUGUSTINE OF HIPPO

One of the effects of God's touch is that it brings to life and consciousness a depth and kind of hunger we never knew we had, that we never knew was possible.

Not satisfaction, mind you, not completion, but *hunger*. God makes his presence known by reminding us of what is absent, what is not yet, what might never be.

We are hungry. We would prefer a God whose touch would take away our hunger. But if we are fortunate, we will go on being hungry.

We burn with desire for a peace that eludes us. We would prefer a God whose touch would flood us with serenity. But if we are fortunate the fire will never go out. Our hope will not die.

"You are hungry for me because I am with you. You desire, because you already have."

LET US PRAY

Here in the weary ending
to a day almost gone,
I would prefer a God whose words
would take away my hunger,
whose touch would flood me with serenity.
I burn with desire
for a peace that eludes me.
Tell me again that I am still hungry
because I am already with you.
I go on desiring you,
because I already have you.
It will be enough, for now,
for this night.

3

Ever ancient, ever new.

—AUGUSTINE OF HIPPO

There is a temptation to freeze God where we were first introduced, to restrict ourselves to first impressions.

Put another way: we are tempted to believe in a God who never grows up, a never changing God, an ever ancient God, a God suitable for display in the hall of antiquities. This is the God who entered our six-year-old imagination as a bearded grandfather and who twenty, forty, sixty years later is still comfortably—or maybe very uncomfortably—with us.

"Ever ancient" gods have their advantages—they never change, they never surprise, they never turn our world upside down. It's the "ever new" God who is full of surprises, challenges, life-rearranging possibilities and propositions.

It may take us a while to find a God who is ever new. Used as we are to our "ancient" version we may pass God on the street without recognizing her. Almost certainly we will begin by looking in all the wrong places—outside, as Augustine discovered. Chances are that we will scan the hours and paths of our lives for a God we can recognize—an ever so ancient God who will be out there, somewhere in the world he created.

But it is, as Augustine says, only when we look within that we will be caught by surprise—by a *beauty ever so ancient and ever so new.*

LET US PRAY

Here in the quiet end to another day,
surprise me with your presence.
Surprise me with a beauty
that is ever new.
Help me to let go
of my childhood
and its comforts.
Show me a new face,
a new beauty,
a new life,
a new self.
Surprise me with who I am.

4

You called, you cried out,
you shattered my deafness.

—AUGUSTINE OF HIPPO

What does God sound like when he calls us, when he cries out for our attention, when his voice needs to be strong enough to cut through the noise to shatter our deafness? What does he look like when he beckons for our attention with beauty strong enough to scatter our blindness?

How can we hear him when our soul is so full of competing loud voices, voices within, voices out there? How will we recognize his voice?

How can we see him when our eyes are captured by the blinding beauty of his creation? How will we recognize his face?

How will we get beyond the sound and the surface to the silence where he waits?

Only by closing our ears to catch the sound of silence.

Only by closing our eyes to catch a glimpse of what cannot be seen.

LET US PRAY

It is so easy to be deaf
to the silence of the night,
so easy to be blind
to what we cannot see.
But here in the fading light of this day,
shatter the noises of my heart,
and release the silence.
Scatter the darkness
that my heart harbors
and release the light
of your presence.

Late have I loved you!

—AUGUSTINE OF HIPPO

Love doesn't come easily or quickly.

To really love is to grow into the full potential of our humanity. It is to leave behind our childhood. It is to hear the life-sized questions for the first time, to respond, to discover, and to accept that in hearing the questions, in embracing love, nothing will ever be the same again.

Chances are that we will come late to such a love. It's not child's play. But however late we love—it will never be too late. There is no "now or never" with love.

For love is not measured in days. There is no bad time for it.

"Imagine," Augustine wrote, "if all creation should become silent, so that we could hear the voice of him who created it. . . ." Creation in time became quiet for Augustine. The same silence awaits us, however late.

LET US PRAY

Late have I listened.
Late have I heard.
Late have I sought.
Late have I found.

Late have I loved you.

But it is not too late.

The Earth

PIERRE TEILHARD DE CHARDIN

All around us,
to right and left,
in front and behind,
above and below,
we have only to go
a little beyond the frontier
of sensible appearances
in order to see the divine
welling up and showing through.
But it is not only close to us,
in front of us,
that the divine presence
is revealed.
It has sprung up universally
and we find ourselves
so surrounded and transfixed by it
that there is no room left
to fall down and adore it,
even within ourselves.

—PIERRE TEILHARD DE CHARDIN

The Divine Milieu

It is almost impossible to write a single line about the vision of Teilhard without being justly accused of misleading simplification. There is no substitute for a close reading of his works. But toward the end of his life he felt impelled to spell out as plainly as he could the forces and ideas that were the driving force of his spiritual life.

> *By means of all created things, without exception, the divine assails us, penetrates us and moulds us. We imagined it as distant and inaccessible, whereas, in fact, we live steeped in its burning layers.* In eo vivimus. *As Jacob said, awakening from his dream, the world, the palpable world, which we were wont to treat with the boredom and disrespect with which we habitually regard places with no sacred association for us, is in truth a holy place and we did not know it.* Venite adoremus.

His is a mysticism grounded in science—a spirituality rooted in the earth.

In a telling vignette—in the course of an Egyptian dig—he picks up a stone, brushes it clean, and is suddenly intensely aware that everything around him is connected in a vast web with God at its center. "God," he writes, "is at work within life. He helps it, raises it up, gives it the impulse that drives it along."

"The deeper I descend into myself, the more I find God at the heart of my being; the more I multiply the links that attach me to things, the more closely does he hold me."

When instead of fleeing the earth we surrender to its embrace, we are rewarded with an incomparable union with the God who is at its heart. It is, ironically, a union with the palpable earth that purifies our union with the spirit.

The world, the earth, is a divine milieu. It is never something to be left behind in our search for God.

Pierre Teilhard de Chardin
(1881-1955)

Pierre Teilhard de Chardin was an ordained Jesuit priest, a theologian, and a world-class paleontologist, a man of extraordinarily original intelligence and profound learning. He was, as many say, the only theologian of his time who was also an established physical scientist and who could live in both worlds as one.

He was a believer unthreatened by anything science might have to say about our human origins and development or by fellow religionists made uncomfortable by his sweep of mind and the daring of his imagination.

His theological and spiritual writings, forbidden publication by the Vatican until after his death in 1955, became international bestsellers. They opened a world of spiritual insight and opportunity to a whole generation of spiritual seekers eager to find a way through walls that separated faith and the science that shaped and underpinned their intellectual and cultural life.

He was born in 1881 in Auvergne, France, into a family of eleven children, to a mother who supported his young piety and to a father who encouraged his young curiosity about the earth. With his father he explored the world around him, climbing its mountains, fishing, hunting, and above all collecting stones and bits and pieces of metal. The world offered nothing "harder, tougher, more durable than this wonderful substance." But, as he wrote in his autobiography, "I can never forget the pathetic depths of a child's despair when I realized one day that iron can be scratched and can rust. . . . I had to look elsewhere for substitutes that would console me."

In time he would be ordained a Jesuit priest, be named professor of geology at the Institut Catholique in Paris, study at the Institute of Human Paleontology at the Museum of Natural History in Paris, and spend nearly twenty-five years in scientific expeditions to China. He would also begin to develop his theological speculation and attract the attention of those it made uncomfortable. He would be forbidden to publish or even speak publicly of his theological ideas, and under such a cloud he would move to New York in 1946 and continue his scientific explorations until he died on Easter Sunday, 1955. His friends, free of any need for ecclesiastical approval, would see to the publication of his books. Fame would follow.

Not everyone would be thrilled by his insights. Many would be put off by the subtlety of his questions and the poetic, scientific density of his language. Some scientists would be angered by his insistence that science and theology are compatible, accusing him of scientific fraud. Still others would be spiritually inspired. New York's governor, Mario Cuomo, would say of him that he made negativism a sin. "He taught us how the whole universe—even pain and imperfection—is sacred."

We have only to go
a little beyond the frontier
of sensible appearances
in order to see the divine.

—PIERRE TEILHARD DE CHARDIN

Only scratch the surface of the earth, Teilhard says, and the divine will well up and show through. It will show through because the divine is there, always there, profoundly there. Our milieu is in fact what Teilhard calls it, divine.

The claim is all the more credible for being not the metaphor of a romantic, but the experience of an established scientist. This is someone who gets his hands dirty digging up the evidence of our human history, someone who looks for our prehistoric footsteps . . . and finds the divine welling up, showing through.

Not only was humanity where he looked, so was God. Not only is God there, but so is the fullness of our humanity.

Only scratch the surface of our life and our humanity will well up and show through. So will God.

LET US PRAY

As this night closes in
show me how to scratch away
its dark and quiet surface
to let the divine,
to let you,
well up in my soul.
Draw me
just beyond what I can see
to where you await.

2

By means of all created things, without exceptions. . . .

—PIERRE TEILHARD DE CHARDIN

There is a persistent tendency in spiritual "circles" to sacrilize some parts of creation and demean everything else as "secular, worldly," as though the creation story had been rewritten to say: "And God made this or that and saw that it was not all that good."

For Teilhard all of creation is sacred. It is "by means of all created things . . . all . . . without exception" that "the divine assails us, penetrates us, and moulds us." The universality of God's presence stretched for Teilhard from the pebbles and stones of his childhood to his unbroken vision of a world permeated by the divine.

There is a parallel tendency to keep the divine at a distance.

For Teilhard, God is close at hand, much closer than we are used to thinking. What we imagined as distant and inaccessible—earth here, God there—is in fact a universe aflame with the burning presence of God.

With Teilhard as a guide we awaken like Jacob from a desacralized world to discover our earth to be a holy place . . . and we did not know it.

LET US PRAY

As this night closes in
help me to realize that
you are as close as the silence and the dark
that surrounds me.

Let me wake
with Jacob
to a realization
that my world
is truly a holy place.

Venite Adoremus.
Come let us adore.
You are here.

3

The divine assails us, penetrates us and moulds us.

—PIERRE TEILHARD DE CHARDIN

For all the silence of God, for all her mystery, the fact is that the divine is daily, hourly assailing us.

It penetrates us and shapes our being. We live in it. It is the air we breathe, the earth we touch and walk on.

It is our roots. When Teilhard talks "earth" he is not using an airy figure of speech, a poetic substitute for the grainy reality of our lives and the world in which we live them. Teilhard at his mystical, poetic best never ceased to be a scientist committed to a measurable, "palpable" world. He did not talk metaphors. He talked the real thing—real God, real earth.

Inclined as we are to believing that spirituality can mean letting "the world go away," Teilhard constantly calls us back to earth reminding us instead that spirituality is about vulnerability. It is about leaving ourselves open to the assaults of the divine.

It is not the kind of language that we find in a child's prayer book.

It is not the God of a well-shaded summer afternoon, but the God of a sun-baked desert dig.

LET US PRAY

As this night closes in
help me to let go
of my need
to control even you.
Assail me with your presence.
Penetrate and shape me.
Let me be vulnerable to your presence,
to your love.
Open my soul.

4

Steep yourself in the sea of matter.

—PIERRE TEILHARD DE CHARDIN

Matter—the physical world—is something that we have been taught to approach gingerly with the hope of controlling it, overcoming it, escaping from its lure.

The message has been: the farther you get from matter the closer you get to God. Then along comes Teilhard to tell us we have been running in the wrong direction.

Just because the spiritual has been aroused in us doesn't mean that we can do without the world. "You hoped that the more thoroughly you rejected the tangible, the closer you would be to spirit; that you would be more divine if you lived in the world of pure thought, or at least more angelic if you fled the corporeal?"

Forget it. Without the material our soul will starve to death. The material world, the earth, is our soul's diet as it reaches ever deeper into the spiritual.

Our hope is not in disembodiment, but in steeping ourselves in the sea of matter.

It is not a matter of escape but of immersion.

LET US PRAY

As this night closes in
let not the dark and the silence
become a hiding place
from this world,
as though I could find you
only by leaving the world behind.
I cannot do
without the world
because I cannot do without you.

5

Let your universal presence spring forth
in a blaze that is at once diaphany and fire.

—PIERRE TEILHARD DE CHARDIN

The presence of the divine: for Teilhard a flame transparent and delicate as a dream, even as it scorches our lives.

For most of us a wall of silence, of unremitting ordinariness. Nothing springs forth. We see no blaze. No great patterns emerge to give the silent earth a voice. There is nothing to break the silence of the journey.

We walk quietly on, God's universal presence an act of faith, our hope warmed by an unfelt blaze.

But the presence of God is no less real for all its silence. It is inseparable from the world around us.

"Bathe yourself in the ocean of matter," Teilhard tells us. "Plunge into it where it is deepest and most violent; struggle in its currents and drink of its waters."

Plunge into the silence that surrounds us.

You will not drown. The pattern that Teilhard sees, though unseen by us, is at work, however quietly, in our lives.

LET US PRAY

As this night closes in
let me not be saddened
by the fire I never see,
by the voice I never hear.
It is enough
to know that it is there.
That you are there.

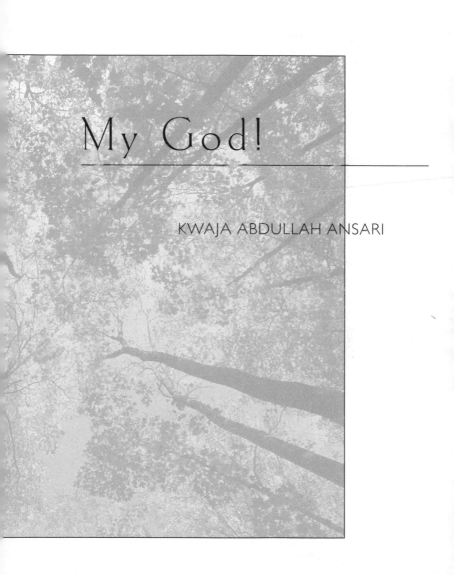

My God!

KWAJA ABDULLAH ANSARI

M<small>y</small> God,
you are merciful in your might,
you are glorious in your beauty,
you are not needful of space,
you require no time.
No one resembles you,
you resemble no one.
It is evident that you are in the soul—
Nay, rather the soul lives
by some thing that you are.

—KWAJA ABDULLAH ANSARI

My God!

When we turn to the spiritual wisdom of a man living over ten centuries ago in a small Persian town it is not a question of spiritual archaeology; nor is it a gnostic journey in search of ancient and esoteric wisdom.

It is a reminder that our challenge is not to invent or reinvent spirituality. Our challenge is to recognize that there are basic, nourishing truths that are both timeless and beyond the sectarian borders that have so often, so deeply, and so perniciously plagued humanity's spiritual journey.

It is a refreshing reminder that no matter where we touch the western mystical tradition there is a shared, enduring wisdom. Certain themes pop to the surface to remind us of what holds us together in our common search, in our common hunger. We are held together by what is timeless, what escapes sectarian boundaries.

We read Kwaja Abdullah Ansari and there is a shock of recognition. Geography, the calendar, personal histories, and religious attachments drop away. We share a common hunger. We are strangers who meet along the way. "I know this man. This man knows me."

We are on a common journey.

For a long time I sought you and found myself.

Now I seek myself and find you.

We pray together.

To find you is our desire

But to comprehend you is beyond our power.

We are companions on the way.

We recognize each other. We recognize ourselves in each other. We recognize God in each other.

My God,
I possess that mirror in which you are reflected
Rather I am that mirror
You are not separate from me.

Kwaja Abdullah Ansari
(c. 1006-1089)

The most popular and significant work by this eleventh-century Islamic mystic—the one that we will meditate on and pray through in the pages that follow—is not one that he wrote. It is a compilation from his various works that was assembled by followers after his death and edited, added to, corrected, even altered over the centuries. No two editions contain the same verses, the same sequence, and the same divisions.

It is called *Munajat,* which means *intimate conversations,* and to this day it is a powerful influence on Islamic mysticism, including Sufism.

There is no question that a principal reason for its survival is its ability to side-step the religious struggle between fundamentalists and theologians that marked his time and his own life and writings—a struggle that remains to this day a source of religious and political tension.

It does so by reminding us that both the literalism of the fundamentalist and the precision of the theologian betray us in our search for a way to talk about the God who is irrevocably beyond language.

The *Munajat* speaks in the language and structures of epigram, poetry, and prayer, recognizing that poetic language is as often as not our most direct route to that which will remain a mystery.

At the same time it remains true to the title given to the collection—by remaining intimate, by remaining conversational. It doesn't hurt that in the hands of Abdullah the poetry and the prayer is often edgy, ironic, and even humorous. In one of his conversations, for example, he prayed:

> *Of your goodness give Abdullah wine,*
> *that his vision be not clouded by his intellect.*

His words are true not just to divine revelation from which he never backs away, but to our human experience and our human emotions, to what we feel when we are in the presence of the mystery that attracts us and which demands our response.

> *I am helpless and perplexed.*
> *Neither have I what I know,*
> *nor know what I have.*

I

My God, I am a stranger.
Make me to know myself.
Give me knowledge of myself, O Lord.

—KWAJA ABDULLAH ANSARI

It is a truism of human love that we start out seeking to know the other and end up coming face to face with a stranger, our self. Abdullah forewarns us that our life with a silent God will follow the same pattern.

The first person we will meet on the spiritual journey will be our self. And we will turn out to be a stranger in need of an introduction, an "unknown person" in need of a name, a question to be answered, a mystery waiting to be explored.

And if we are not careful we will turn out to be an all but insuperable obstacle on our path. Our lack of self-knowledge will stand between us and our hunger to know God.

We will have to get out of the way. But until we accept the fact that we are in the way the path will remain blocked. The stranger will have to go. The unknown person will have to be named. Before we get to know God, we will have to get to know our self a lot better than we do. It's the first stop on the journey. We take it in hope.

LET US PRAY

My God,

more than anything else this night

I pray to know myself,

lest I remain a stranger to myself

and to you.

Make me to know myself.

Give me knowledge of myself, O Lord.

2

My God, I left behind the whole world to search for you.
But you were the whole world, and I could not see it.

—KWAJA ABDULLAH ANSARI

It's not just that we tend to look for God in all the wrong places, or that we overlook God where he is. It is getting over the notion that we can locate God. Or that we need to.

It is a case of recognizing that God is not here or there in the world, or even everywhere. God is the world in which we live.

God is our environment. She is the air we breathe. And because we are for the most part no more conscious of God than we are of our own breath, it becomes a matter of reflection, of pausing long enough to remember: "I am breathing. I am in God. God is in me."

It is evident that you are in the soul—
Nay, rather the soul lives by some thing that you are.

We are not God. But we are inseparable from God.

My God,
I possess that mirror in which you are reflected
Rather I am that mirror
You are not separate from me.

LET US PRAY

My God,

for a long time I sought you and found myself

Now I seek myself and find you.

You were stealthily apparent, and I unaware.

You were hidden in my breast and I unaware.

To the exclusion of all the world

I sought you openly.

You were the whole world and I unaware.

Now I seek myself and find you.

3

We are forbidden to despair.

—KWAJA ABDULLAH ANSARI

There is often in the writings of the great mystics an edge of garden-variety bargaining that on occasion they put at the service of very spiritual objectives. Sometimes there is humor, even irony. Teresa of Avila had this touch. So does Abdullah.

We are forbidden to despair, he writes, because God has said that he is merciful.

There is an edge to this intimate conversation with God. "You made a promise," he is saying to God, "we are going to hold you to it. In a world where hope can seem foolish, where trust is so regularly misplaced, we have your word that you are merciful. We'll take you at your word."

There are those, of course, who will say that this kind of conversation with God diminishes God, eats away at the mystery of God and his absolute incomprehensibility. But the fact is that we do not lose our humanity as we approach God and his mystery.

Our still human heart yearns for security, for someone to trust, for some reason not to despair.

> *My God, you are not a merchant.*
> *Have mercy on us, gratis.*

LET US PRAY

My God,

You have said that you are generous.

Therein lies all my hope.

Since you have said that you are merciful,

I will not lose hope,

I will not despair.

Hear the prayer of my heart.

Give my soul permission to hope.

4

·My God, You are not needful of space.
You require no time.

—KWAJA ABDULLAH ANSARI

God is both within and beyond the time and space that is our home. She transcends both and requires neither. With her there is no "was," no "will be." God simply is. Here and now. Always in the present tense.

This means that everything God does for us is already done. The best we can do is to catch our self up whenever we start limiting God to our categories, to our time, to our space.

When we say, for example, that our spiritual growth will "take time" we are saying only that it will take time for our soul, for our life, for our practice to catch up and respond to what already is. Wherever we seek to go, God is already there. Whatever we dream of is already accomplished, already true.

Whatever is to be done, is being done, is already done.

God, however, works with our humanity even as she works within it. She doesn't rush us. She honors our need for the space and time so that we can recognize, absorb, and respond to what she is accomplishing in our lives.

God is patient with us, even when we are impatient with ourselves.

LET US PRAY

My God,
be patient with me
as I struggle
to become
who I already am,
to do for myself
what you have already done for me.
Help me to understand
when I look for you
that you are already here.

5

I am helpless and perplexed.
Neither have I what I know
nor know what I have.

—KWAJA ABDULLAH ANSARI

Most, if not all, of us who have at some point considered ourselves to be persons of faith have also believed in the same breath that this was synonymous with being persons of certitude.

But the truth is much closer to what Abdullah says. God does not play the role of answer man in our lives. We are as likely to feel perplexed as certain, as likely to feel helpless as powerful. Hope is not about certainty, but about living and growing in the eye of mystery, about living without "answers" in the face of those questions that go to the core of what it means to be human.

Is there a God? Is there an afterlife?

These are the questions that take us where certainty is a stranger.

Hope is not about having better or even any answers, but about an ever-deepening acceptance that it is how we live with what is unknowable and unanswerable that gives depth to our lives. "I neither have what I know nor know what I have."

But I have hope.

And it is enough.

LET US PRAY

My God,
sleep may come easier
to those who are certain,
to those who have answers.
But this is not where I find myself.
As darkness settles over my day,
I am soul deep
in the mysteries that surround me,
that beckon me where certitude is a stranger.
I cannot settle for answers
when it is you
I seek.

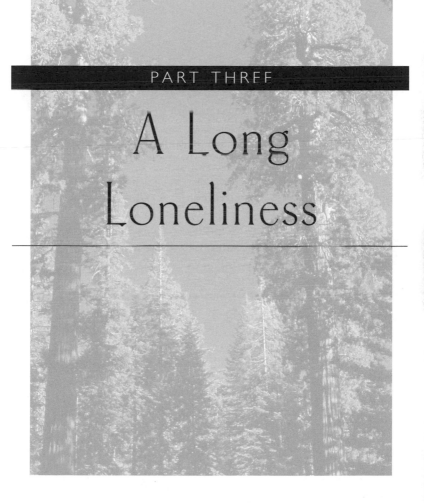

PART THREE

A Long
Loneliness

"Even as a child of six," Dorothy Day recalled much later, "I often awakened in the dark and felt the blackness and terror of nonbeing. I do not know whether I knew anything of death, but these were two terrors I experienced as a child, terror of silence and loneliness and a sense of Presence, awful and mysterious."

**

At the very heart of our humanity—and therefore at the heart of our spiritual journey—there is, in the words of Dorothy Day, a long loneliness, an otherness that is no more a matter of physical isolation than the silence of God is an absence of sound.

It is a solitude that God will not, cannot take away.

This solitude is not physical. It is not the solitude of a cell, nor the solitude of a mountain trail. It is not a passing condition that can be exchanged or adopted at will, but rather a fundamental spiritual truth about our existence, a key to our spiritual identity that we dare not avoid or deny if we are ever to satisfy our hunger for God.

We walk with God. But we are not God. We may be surrounded by companions and supported by them at every step. But we walk alone. Our soul aches with an unbridgeable loneliness.

We are persons. The heart of who we are, our personhood, is—in the startling phrase of the medieval theologians—that which is "radically incommunicable." No matter how hard we try, no matter how deep our desire, we cannot erase the "otherness" that separates us.

Our spirituality is rooted in this mystery. It takes its shape in this mystery. It flowers in this mystery.

Not only can I not undo the mystery of God's otherness, I cannot undo my own otherness or the otherness of my fellow travelers. I am not, nor can I become my father or mother, not my brother or sister, not my lover, not my spouse with whom I am one flesh, not even the child whom I have brought to birth, to whom I have given breath and flesh and history. I am not he. I am not she. I am not you. Nor am I anyone else.

I am this incredibly mysterious, incommunicable reality: a person.

I am "I."

It is an uneasy discovery that takes us where we are not always prepared to go.

"I" can feel empty and afraid, alone and threatened, insecure in an ambiguous and often cruel universe. I can feel, as Dorothy Day did, a "terror of silence and loneliness."

Or "I" can celebrate and explore the inescapable mystery into which we have been born—the mystery of God's silence, of his otherness, the mysterious otherness of those to whom we are the closest. For we are destined to grow in mystery and with it. We fall in love with the mystery of others. We make love to their otherness. We marry their mystery. We conceive another. We give birth to mystery.

But we will never cease to be "I." They will never cease to be "you." God will never cease to be the ultimate other.

We may embrace each other with the hope of reaching beyond our separate solitudes only to be brought up short by a reminder that we are human, that we are persons, that the core of who we are is not communicable, nor is the core of those we love.

We look across our dinner table to a partner who may have been there for decades and we suddenly realize that as much as we know about each other, there is a central core to the "other" that is beyond our knowing and our sharing. We cannot in the end penetrate the mystery of the other. We cannot dissolve it. There is a line we cannot cross.

There is that moment when parents turn to each other and wonder aloud at the miraculous presence of a child who is undeniably, mysteriously a real and separate person. The child may be two. The child may be twenty. "Where do you suppose she came from?" The mystery grows and never lessens. It's a "puzzlement."

We brush against each other, loving each other, hoping that this overwhelming mystery will surrender to our need to know and be known, but knowing that not even love can ultimately penetrate and capture the mystery of the other, or our own otherness.

In the end we all die our own death.

But with each mysterious encounter with otherness we unlock more of our soul, experience more deeply our hunger. We come to know better the nature of our solitude.

We sense with Dorothy Day a "presence, awful and mysterious." We want a taste of God, the ultimate other who alone measures up to the depth of our solitude, who is not put off by our otherness, who never asks us or expects us to be other than we are, to be other than who we are, who will never require that we resolve the conflicts and contradictions of our life before we are acceptable.

So we come bearing the only gift we have to give— our personhood, our solitude, our otherness, our hope.

***

This talk of solitude and "radical incommunicability" can easily come off as bloodless word games or as pop psychology all dressed up as God talk—but it is neither.

It is a central and profound insight into our humanity with consequences that color even our most bread-and-butter spiritual efforts.

Only when we think of solitude—our incommunicability—as the root of our uniqueness can we begin to understand its role in our spirituality, how basic it is to developing a realistic and fulfilling spiritual life, how critical it is to our hope.

For one thing, God's invitation is always to come as we are, to come as only we can be; not as a note of divine courtesy and understanding, but as a recognition and celebration of our humanity, our personhood, our otherness. We don't have to be Mother Teresa to get a hearing. We don't have to be anyone other than who we are—black, brown, white, yellow, gay, straight, married, single, divorced, old, young, whatever.

But if you are like many of us, there have been and still are moments when you are tempted to believe that to be spiritually acceptable you need to be someone else. You think that the serious spiritual seeker needs different skills and different passions from yours. You would be better off if you were from a different, less dysfunctional family at some other moment in time, with a different history and different failures.

We hobble ourselves with a notion that somewhere out there is something called a saint, an approved spiritual creature, and the purpose of our spiritual journey is to imitate, even become, that person.

But the purpose of our spirituality is to recognize, accept, and celebrate our own uniquely mysterious and miraculous personhood. We are who we are and that's not only good enough, it is all that is possible. We are not beings rolled off an assembly line. We are persons.

God is not expecting someone else. We may be disappointed with God, but she will not be disappointed when we show up trailing our history. She never is.

But here's the thing. We have to be willing and prepared to bring our whole self to the table. All of our sad and spotted history. Not just the stuff that makes us look good, like we think a saint should look, but the imperfect stuff, the bad stuff, even the weird stuff—all the stuff that makes us who we are and not someone else.

Solid spirituality is not built on an edited version of our selves, a Playboy photo, all our blemishes air-brushed out, all our good features highlighted.

Nor is a spiritual life one that has been reduced to the original, factory equipped model, all the optional accessories removed, accident records buried (even "head-ons" and "close-to-totaled" ones), dents and scratches bumped out and painted over—no trace of where we have been and how we got here.

Instead it is a life that accepts and celebrates the fact that as shopworn and damaged as we may be, we are who we are and what may not be good enough for us, for our families, or for our friends is good enough for God.

Who we are is a person, an incommunicable mystery, not a face in the crowd, not someone who can be mistaken for anyone else. We are one of a kind. We are the one that God, however silent, awaits.

We are those who in the face of God's silence go on hoping.

****

My journey brought me one late summer night to a memory-drenched lake house, to the mustiness of an old familiar room.

As I had hoped, nothing had changed—not the old room's patch of fireplace light, nor its not-quite-adequate warmth, and most certainly not the sound of familiar voices rehashing dreams and disappointments.

This room was "home" and I was preparing to leave it behind. It was important to me to keep the fire stoked, to keep the conversation going, to hold on as long as I could to what I had. I remember thinking that the alternative was the darkness beyond the closed doors that led outside, the chill of the damp lake air, the uneven, slippery, unlighted steps. Silence and a long loneliness.

And for a while, at least, words were in control of the night. I could go on believing, if just for a moment, that this familiar room was the world, that it was all that I needed, that all I hungered for was here, that there was still some way of avoiding the darkness, the silence, and the unknown beyond its walls.

But at some point someone would have said: "It's getting late   " We would have run out of words. It would be time to find our way into the dark, moonless night, a small, flickering flashlight in hand—a flashlight that could illumine not much more than a single step in front of us.

I had come here wanting to believe that there was some way to avoid the solitude and the silence, the mystery beyond familiarity.

But I knew that sooner or later I would have to welcome the unknown and the uncontrollable. I would have to leave behind the room's familiarity and comfort, exchanging them for the long and lonely silence on the other side of the door.

My life with a silent God would have to begin again in hope.

As it often had. As it still does.

You Might Want to Read . . .

Where Only Love Can Go (The Cloud of Unknowing)—John Kirvan

God in Search of Man—Abraham Heschel

Life of the Soul: Julian of Norwich—Edmund College

Dietrich Bonhoeffer—Robert Coles

The Long Loneliness—Dorothy Day

God Awaits You (Meister Eckhart)—Richard Chilson

Charles de Foucauld—Robert Ellsberg

Saint Augustine—Gary Wills

Pierre Teilhard de Chardin—Ursula King

Islam: A Short History—Karen Armstrong

Visit us at:
www.sorinbooks.com

To learn more about the author and his other books contact
www.johnkirvan.com